Awakening to the Heartbeat of God

Servants of Christ and stewards of the mysteries of God

Awakening to the Heartbeat of God

Harvesting Souls

by

Susan C. Skelley

All scripture quotations are from the
Authorized King James Version of the Bible.

AWAKENING TO THE HEARTBEAT OF GOD
Copyright © 2007—by Susan C. Skelley
ALL RIGHTS RESERVED

No part of this book may be reproduced or transmitted in any form or by any means, electronic or mechanical, including photocopying, recording or by any information retrieval system.

Original cover design by Sherie Campbell
sonandshield@comcast.net

Published by:

McDougal & Associates
P.O. Box 194
Greenwell Springs, LA 70739-0194
www.thepublishedword.com

McDougal & Associates is dedicated to the spreading of the Gospel of Jesus Christ to as many people as possible in the shortest time possible.

ISBN 13: 978-0-9777053-5-1
ISBN 10: 0-9777053-5-8
Printed in the United States of America
For Worldwide Distribution

Acknowledgments

Thank you—such simple words—yet no amount of words could adequately express the gratitude and thankfulness I have toward the many people who have encouraged me, prayed for me, assisted me and imparted to me all that was needed to make this book become a reality. Thank you, with the heartfelt prayer that our heavenly Father will touch your life in many special ways.

To my family, especially Darryl and Danny, my sons: I love all of you so much!

To Helen, Harold, Jane, Inez, Stephanie, Clarence, Bill, Robert, Ethel, Roger, Louis, Molly and Bill, Matthew, Lydia, Daisy, Judy, Jessica (go Kaizen Blitz!) and Chuck (you live on in the hearts of all those who have loved you), and you remind us that a great cloud of witnesses is there to continually cheer us on.

To friends, the long established ones, as well as the new ones: You have been the gold and silver of my life.

To those very special friends: Paula (for all of your typing), Martha Jo and Vicki (for reviewing the book and offering suggestions), Mary Beth (Sad Heart, Happy Heart!) and to all the other friends who took the time to listen to ideas by phone, review portions of writing, assist with computer questions and format, lift my arms in prayer and simply believe with me for the vision! Be blessed, my friends!

To my co-workers: We have worked together through many seasons of life. You are all blessings! (Got chocolate? Well, maybe a few carrots!)

To Spirit Life Harvest Church, especially Pastors Ken and Laura Hope: Thank you for teaching me what it means to love and worship our heavenly Father.

To Daytona City Church, especially Pastors Donnie and Linda and Pastors Rodney and Kathy Tolleson: I am continually learning to stretch and grow under your leadership! To Kelly: Thank you for your patience with my frequent phone calls to the church. To Pastor Greg: Thank you for perseverance with the computer, corrections and for guiding me with computer issues.

To the Body of Christ in Volusia County: I have learned so much from so many of you. May our Lord Jesus Christ continue to grow us, unite us, and prepare us for revival—seven times greater than we can even imagine! We shall see miracles, and we shall have a mighty harvest!

To my heavenly Father, His precious Son Jesus and our wonderful Counselor, the Holy Spirit: Thank You for all of the ways Your heartbeat is demonstrated in our everyday life! I am so thankful that Your heart beats for each and every soul!

The harvest truly is great, but the labourers are few: pray ye therefore the Lord of the harvest that he would send forth labourers into his harvest. Luke 10:2

For God so loved the world, that he gave his only begotten Son, that whosoever believeth in him should not perish, but have everlasting life. John 3:16

The fruit of the righteous is a tree of life; and he that winneth souls is wise. Proverbs 11:30

For I am not ashamed of the gospel of Christ: for it is the power of God unto salvation to every one that believeth; to the Jew first, and also to the Greek. Romans 1:16

And Jesus came and spake unto them, saying, All power is given unto me in heaven and in earth. Go ye therefore, and teach all nations, baptizing them in the name of the Father, and of the Son, and of the Holy Ghost. Matthew 28:18-19

But ye shall receive power, after that the Holy Ghost is come upon you: and ye shall be witnesses unto me both in Jerusalem, and in all Judea, and in Samaria, and unto the uttermost part of the earth. Acts 1:8

Whosoever therefore shall confess me before men, him will I confess also before my Father which is in heaven. Matthew 10:32

Wherefore I put thee in remembrance that thou stir up the gift of God, which is in thee by the putting on of my hands. For God hath not given us the spirit of fear; but of power, and of love, and of a sound mind. Be not thou therefore ashamed of the testimony of our Lord. 2 Timothy 1:6-8

For the preaching of the cross is to them that perish foolishness; but unto us which are saved it is the power of God. 1 Corinthians 1:18

Jesus saith unto him, Feed my sheep. John 21:17

Let him know, that he which converteth the sinner from the error of his way, shall save a soul from death, and shall hide a multitude of sins. James 5:20

The Spirit of the Lord is upon me, because he hath anointed me to preach the gospel to the poor; he hath sent me to heal the brokenhearted, to preach deliverance to the captives, and recovering of sight to the blind, to set at liberty them that are bruised, To preach the acceptable year of the Lord. Luke 4:18-19

Herein is my Father glorified, that ye bear much fruit; so shall ye be my disciples. John 15:8

For the preaching of the cross is to them that perish foolishness; but unto us which are saved, it is the power of God. 1 Corinthians 1:18

And I looked, and behold a white cloud, and upon the cloud one sat like unto the Son of man, having on his head a golden crown, and in his hand a sharp sickle. And another angel came out of the temple, crying with a loud voice to him that sat on the cloud, Thrust in thy sickle, and reap: for the time is come for thee to reap; for the harvest of the earth is ripe. And he that sat on the cloud thrust in his sickle on the earth; and the earth was reaped. Revelations 14:14-16

Feed the flock of God which is among you, taking the oversight thereof, not by constraint, but willingly; not for filthy lucre, but of a ready mind; neither as being lords over God's heritage, but being ensamples to the flock. And when the chief Shepherd shall appear, ye shall receive a crown of glory that fadeth not away. 1 Peter 5:2-4

And how shall they preach, except they be sent? as it is written, How beautiful are the feet of them that preach the gospel of peace, and bring glad tidings of good things! Romans 10:15

And he [Jesus] saith unto them, Follow me, and I will make you fishers of men. Matthew 4:19

Contents

Foreword by Pastors Rodney and Kathy Tolleson .. 11
Foreword by Pastor Kenneth Hope 12
How This Material Can Be Used 13

Introduction 17

Part I: Basics for Reaching Souls 19
  1. Who Reached Out to You? 21
  2. Know Your Harvest Fields 25
  3. Power to Witness 29
  4. Do You Know Him as Lord of the Harvest? 33
  5. Preparing the Ground 37
  6. An Overcoming Witness 41
  7. The Gospel in a Nutshell 45
  8. Sad Heart, Happy Heart 49
  9. Taking a Walk on the Roman Road 53
 10. What Will You Give Up to See Captives Set Free? .. 57
 11. Hospitality, Jesus' Style 61
 12. Prayer Evangelism 65
 13. A Harvest Requires Light 69
 14. Prepare Their Hearts, Lord, with Our Words 73
 15. "But I Don't Like Persecution" 77
 16. Too Good Not to Share 81

Part II: Dealing with Special Challenges 85
 17. "I've Sinned Too Much to Be Saved" 87
 18. "I'll Accept Christ 'Later' " 91

19. "The Church Is Full of Hypocrites" 95
20. "I Just Can't Change" 99
21. "I'll Lose All My Friends" 103
22. "But I'm Not Living Right" 107

Part III: Tearing Down Specific Strongholds 111
23. "I'm About As Good As Anyone Else" 113
24. "I Do Good Things for the Community" 117
25. "I Already Belong to a Church" 121
26. "It All Sounds So Foolish" 125
27. "It Didn't Work for Me" 129
28. "How Do I Know That What the Bible Says Is True?" .. 133
29. "Help! I Have Unforgiveness" 137
30. "If God Is So Good, Why Do So Many Bad Things Happen in the World?" 141

Part IV: Putting on Daddy's Shoes 145
31. Shoes of Faith 147
32. Shoes of Christlike Character 151
33. The Shoes of a Warrior 155
34. Shoes of Victory 159

Part V: Nurturing New Babies 163
35. The Miracle of New Birth 165
36. Feed Them 169
37. Encourage them to Submit to Water Baptism 173
38. Encourage them to Receive the Baptism of the Holy Spirit 177
39. Teach Them to Pray 181
40. Give Them Room to Grow 185

    Epilogue 189

    Ministry Page 192

Foreword by Pastors Rodney and Kathy Tolleson

Awakening to the Heartbeat of God is a unique daily devotional which not only encourages meditation on the teachings of the Word of God related to evangelism, but it also offers a prescription for action. The Bible says that we are to be *"doers of the Word"* (James 1:22), and that's why this book is so special. It takes the reader beyond mere theories and into the actual experience of winning souls.

The very last words Jesus spoke on earth bid us to go and spread the Good News and to make disciples, yet often we don't know where to start. This book can help. We believe that as you read *Awakening to the Heartbeat of God* you will develop the motivation and skills to become a great soulwinner. As Jesus said, *"The harvest truly is plentiful, but the labourers are few"* (Matthew 9:37). We can all make a difference by getting involved in evangelism.

Sue Skelley is enthusiastic about soulwinning and is a dedicated minister in the marketplace. We're very proud of her and of this, her first literary accomplishment. We know that this book has been (and will continue to be) a blessing to the Body of Christ because it's such a great tool for individuals and for evangelistic teams. We hope that you are changed, challenged and charged by reading it.

Rodney and Kathy Tolleson, Senior Ministers
Daytona City Church, Daytona Beach, Florida

Foreword by Pastor Kenneth Hope

Having known Sue Skelley for many years, I can say that *Awakening to the Heartbeat of God* is a book of life experience. This author has taken a journey with the Lord that is reflected beautifully on every page. Faith cannot truly be taught as much as it is caught, and Sue has captured the essence of what her heart has taken in over the years, and this has made her qualified to impart the same to her readers.

As I have known Sue as her pastor, I have long been aware of her desire to win souls and see them nurtured and discipled into the Body of Christ. In these pages, she conveys this call in a way that challenges the reader to draw near to Christ and then to reach out to the world He came to deliver. Some may consider the material on these pages to be the nuts and bolts of the Christian life. I see it more as steps on an awesome journey that can take every believer from season to season and from glory to glory.

May these devotions bring you hope, encouragement and renewed confidence. Allow this study to cause you to become fully aware that the same God who has transformed your heart is the One who will guide you through every joy and challenge along the way to the complete fulfillment of His great destiny in your life. May the Lord bless you with each step as you are taken to the next level of the Lord's abounding grace and great favor over your life.

Rev. Kenneth S. Hope, Sr., Senior Pastor,
Spirit Life Harvest Church, Daytona Beach, Florida

How This Material Can Be Used

The purpose of this book is to spark the Christian believers to become firecrackers and dynamite for God's Kingdom, rediscovering His greatest miracle: the salvation of the human soul! The harvest field is plentiful, requiring effective evangelistic teaching to be now multiplied throughout the Body of Christ.

Although the material is organized in a 40-day devotional style, allow the Holy Spirit to lead you through the process. The material can be used for individual devotions, small group Bible studies, evangelistic seminars or as an evangelism tool for any group wanting to be better equipped. This is an effective tool that any church can utilize during seasons of prayer and fasting. Church members who commit to reading the book during such seasons can expect a fresh outpouring of the spirit of evangelism, as well as increased enthusiasm and faith for reaching the souls in their harvest fields.

The book contains 40 devotions, with 5 specific topic sections:

* *Basics for Reaching Souls*
* *Dealing with Special Challenges*
* *Tearing Down Specific Strongholds*
* *Putting on Daddy's Shoes (equipping to go into the harvest fields with victory)*

* Nurtuting New Babies (establishing new believers in their faith)

The hope is that each section will better equip individuals, Bible study groups and churches to identify their harvest fields and use the tools described throughout the book to reach them. The outcome will be an increase of willing laborers who will be used by our heavenly Father to reach souls for His Kingdom.

Each of the 40 devotions is organized into 5 sections:

The Devotion: This section provides a scripture lesson to help motivate and equip believers to identify the people in their specific harvest fields and to them "go forth," impacting these individuals for Christ. All Christians are called to share the Good News of Christ to those around them. These lessons impart faith, encouragement and confidence, helping each reader to become a more effective soulwinner.

Scripture Keys to Declare: Romans 10:17 teaches us *"faith cometh by hearing, and hearing by the word of God."* The scripture keys are intended to be spoken out loud, declared into the atmosphere. Whether they are spoken by individuals or groups of individuals, the outcome will be an increase of faith that the harvest fields will be impacted by your witness.

Activity/Response Section: This book is intended to multiply the spirit of evangelism throughout the Body of Christ. The activity/response section is meant to encourage each reader to become a more effective "doer" of the Word. The varied activities help readers identify harvest fields, use effective evangelism tools, pray with a heartbeat for specific souls and tear down strongholds that would otherwise hinder salvation. The result? More believers will become willing witnesses for the Lord of the Harvest. They will also experience the joy of seeing souls drawn out of darkness and into God's glorious Kingdom of light.

My Prayer from the Heart: This section is meant to personalize each topic of evangelism into prayer with our true source of power, our Lord and Savior, Jesus Christ. Although each devotion contains a written prayer, the hope is that each reader will spend more time praying from his or her own heart, as he or she is led by the Holy Spirit.

The Lord's Answer/s to Me: This section is meant to encourage readers to hear what the Lord is speaking to their hearts. Listen to His guidance and follow through with faith. Before long, you, too, will be awakened to His heartbeat for souls, and you will be led by His Holy Spirit to be a powerful witness for Christ.

My prayer for you is that your heart will truly open to a greater relationship with our heavenly Father, His Son Jesus and His Holy Spirit. I pray that you will have a greater sensitivity to His heartbeat for souls. I remember years ago hearing the Father say that He does not give up on anyone. He loved the entire world so much that He gave us His Son Jesus, as Lord and Savior for all. As we remember our own experience of salvation, may we also receive God's heartbeat for souls, a heart that beats continuously and does not give up on anyone. Take His hand, listen for His heartbeat, identify the harvest fields that He desires to send you to and then go forth!

INTRODUCTION

Have you ever taken time from this very hectic world to stop and really listen to God's heartbeat? It overwhelms me to consider His heart, for it is so pure and so compassionate, full of tender mercy and forgiveness, so holy, and yet so approachable through the precious blood of Jesus Christ. God's Word assures us that His heart reaches out to the entire world, and yet each of us is given the freedom to receive His love, through Jesus Christ, or to reject it. He chooses us, and yet each of us is given the choice of whether or not to choose Him.

What do you remember about that miraculous day when *you* opened the door of *your* heart to the Lord Jesus Christ and to the heart of our heavenly Father? My experience could be compared to that of a newly born infant. Somehow I knew that my life was forever changed, and my deepest desire became and has continued to be to remain close to the heartbeat of my heavenly Father.

Listen closely to His heartbeat today. Tune your ears to go beyond every teaching and revelation you have ever learned from God's Word in the past. Although those teachings are important and transforming, we need to listen ever so closely to see what is at the very core of His heart. His loving, compassionate heart is beating for you and for me and, indeed, for every living soul.

Every time someone extends the love of Jesus to another

person, you can hear the heartbeat of God in the process. His heartbeat grows stronger, with pure love, for each soul saved—whether here in Daytona Beach, in New York City, in China or Africa or in the smallest island in the world. Whether they are rich or poor, and whatever color they happen to be, the heart of God beats steadily for souls everywhere. And our heavenly Father asks you today, "Will you reflect My heartbeat and allow Me to thrust you into the harvest fields around you?"

Does your heart beat for souls? Do you rejoice with the angels in Heaven over one sinner who repents, turning his or her life over to Jesus? In the following pages, you will be given many opportunities to hear and respond to the heartbeat of God. May He open your eyes to His Word and to your harvest fields, and may He reveal to you that evangelism is simply being a willing vessel through which God can draw others to Himself, through His loving kindness—His heartbeat.

I pray that *Awakening to the Heartbeat of God* will forever change you. May your heart beat for souls and may you bear much fruit for God's Kingdom. Be blessed as you willingly enter the harvest fields that our heavenly Father has prepared for you. Are you ready for the journey? Then take His hand and listen for His heartbeat. And now, let the journey begin.

Susan C. Skelley
Port Orange, Florida

Part I

Basics for Reaching Souls

Day 1

Who Reached Out to You?

For God so loved the world that he gave his only begotten Son, that WHOSOEVER believeth in him should not perish, but have everlasting life.

John 3:16, Emphasis Added

Before you make a commitment to reach out to others with the love of Christ, allow the Holy Spirit to remind you of the people, prayers and testimonies that were used to bring *you* to that special moment when you asked Jesus to be your Lord and Savior. Most importantly, think of Jesus, God's only Son, and think of His sacrifice on the cross.

When Jesus was crucified on the cross, He submitted to pain, humiliation, suffering and death—all because He had *you* on His mind. Throughout my walk with the Lord, I've often heard the phrase: "If you had been the only person in the world who needed a Savior, Jesus would still have gone to the cross." That's how deep the love of our Lord Jesus reaches. It's for you, for me and for the entire world!

Now, think of the people who told you about Jesus. Because they willingly allowed Him to shine through them, God used them to bring you out of darkness and into His glorious *"light"* (Acts 26:18). Who were the people who were not *"ashamed"* to tell you about the Lord and His salvation

Awakening to the Heartbeat of God

(Romans 1:16)? Can you recall relatives, friends or neighbors who seemed to pray fervently for you? God used willing laborers to draw you into His Kingdom and perhaps others to teach you and help you grow in your walk with the Lord. Now, will *you* be willing to be used to draw others and to teach them? God will equip you with His wisdom and His guidance.

SCRIPTURE KEYS TO DECLARE

Acts 26:18:
To open their eyes, and to turn them from darkness to light, and from the power of Satan unto God, that they may receive forgiveness of sins, and inheritance among them which are sanctified by faith that is in me.

Colossians 1:13:
Who hath delivered us from the power of darkness, and hath translated us into the kingdom of his dear Son.

Romans 1:16:
For I am not ashamed of the gospel of Christ: for it is the power of God unto salvation to every one that believeth; to the Jew first, and also to the Greek.

Proverbs 11:30:
The fruit of the righteous is a tree of life; and he that winneth souls is wise.

Harvesting Souls

POINTS TO PONDER

Who and What Do You Remember About Your Own Salvation?

1. Describe the day you asked Jesus to be your Lord and Savior. What do you remember most about Him?
   _____
   _____
   _____

2. Who were the key people who told you about Jesus and how did our heavenly Father use them to reach out to you?
   _____
   _____
   _____

3. List people who have discipled you to grow in your walk with Jesus.
   _____
   _____
   _____

4. Who has prayed for you through the years?
   _____
   _____
   _____

My Prayer from the Heart

Heavenly Father,

Help me to co-labor with You to evangelize and disciple. As You, heavenly Father, used willing people to reach out to *me*, help me to now reach out to others. Give me a heart for people, a heart that desires all people everywhere to know You as Lord and Savior. And open my eyes and heart to the opportunities to share Jesus with those around me.

In Jesus' name,

The Lord's Answer/s to Me

_____

_____

_____

_____

Day 2

Know Your Harvest Fields

Say not ye, there are yet four months, and then cometh harvest? behold, I say unto YOU, lift up YOUR eyes, and look on the fields; for they are white already to harvest.   John 4:35, Emphasis Added

Did you know that there's a harvest field especially prepared for *you*? What is God trying to tell you in His Word? He's telling you that there are people ready to receive Jesus now! More specifically, He's telling you that there are people you know who are ready to receive Him now! And to reach them, God wants to use you.

Why is this true? Simply because God has prepared the hearts of people around you to listen to you, and He's preparing your heart to become a willing witness to them. Jesus told His disciples: *"The harvest truly is plenteous, but the labourers are few; pray ye therefore the Lord of the harvest, that he will send forth labourers into his harvest"* (Matthew 9:37-38).

Now is the time to tell the Lord, as Isaiah, "Here am I; send me!"

SCRIPTURE KEYS TO DECLARE

Isaiah 6:8:
*Also I heard the voice of the L*ORD*, saying, whom shall I send, and who will go for us? Then said I, Here am I; send me.*

Matthew 28:18-20:
And Jesus came and spake unto them, saying, All power is given unto me in heaven and in earth. Go ye therefore, and teach all nations, baptizing them in the name of the Father, and of the Son, and of the Holy Ghost; teaching them to observe all things whatsoever I have commanded you: and, lo, I am with you alway, even unto the end of the world.

Harvesting Souls

POINTS TO PONDER

How Can You Know Your Harvest Fields?

1. Make a list of family, co-workers and friends who need a personal relationship with Jesus Christ.
   _____
   _____
   _____
   _____

2. When Jesus sends us into our harvest fields, He promises to be with us, guiding us in our words and actions. How has Jesus helped you to reach out to other people?
   _____
   _____
   _____
   _____

3. How is the Holy Spirit prompting and equipping you to reach out to others with your words and actions?
   _____
   _____
   _____
   _____

My Prayer from the Heart

Heavenly Father,

As You show me the harvest fields in my life, show me what to say and do to be an effective witness for You. Prepare the hearts of those who need my witness, and work through me as You draw my family, friends and co-workers (my personal harvest field) closer to Your Kingdom.

In Jesus' name,

The Lord's Answer/s to Me

Day 3

Power to Witness

But ye shall receive power, after that the Holy Ghost is come upon you: and ye shall be witnesses unto me both in Jerusalem and in all Judea, and in Samaria, and unto the uttermost part of the earth.   Acts 1:8

Jesus knew that effective evangelism would require a power greater than our own. He willingly imparts to us the power we need to teach others about Him. Before He sent out the disciples He had personally mentored to do this work of soulwinning, He said to them: *"All power is given unto me in heaven and in earth. Go ye therefore, and teach all nations, ... teaching them to observe all things whatsoever I have commanded you."* (Matthew 28:18-20). So Jesus has *"all power,"* and He is willing to share that power with us so that we can be effective witnesses for Him. This power comes to us through the baptism of the Holy Spirit and equips us with both the enablement and the sensitivity required to witness about our Lord Jesus wherever and whenever the Spirit should lead us.

Regularly praying in the Holy Spirit also keeps us filled with the love of Jesus so that we may reach out to others with His heart of compassion. So don't be afraid. Trust the Lord and His power in you for those He leads you to speak with concerning salvation. He will fill you with the words, wisdom and power to effectively reach those around you. (*For more details on the baptism of the Holy Spirit, see Day 38.)

SCRIPTURE KEYS TO DECLARE

Acts 1:8:
But ye shall receive power, after that the Holy Ghost is come upon you: and ye shall be witnesses unto me both in Jerusalem and in all Judea, and in Samaria, and unto the uttermost part of the earth.

Mark 16:15-18:
And he [Jesus] said unto them, Go ye into all the world, and preach the gospel to every creature. He that believeth and is baptized shall be saved; but he that believeth not shall be damned. And these signs shall follow them that believe; In my name shall they cast out devils; they shall speak with new tongues; they shall take up serpents; and if they drink any deadly thing, it shall not hurt them; they shall lay hands on the sick, and they shall recover.

Jude 20-22:
But ye, beloved, building up yourselves on your most holy faith, praying in the Holy Ghost, keep yourselves in the love of God, looking for the mercy of our Lord Jesus Christ unto eternal life. And of some have compassion, making a difference.

Harvesting Souls

POINTS TO PONDER

Simple Steps that Produce a Powerful Witness

1. Here are some simple steps for reaching out to others:
   - Offer to pray for someone in need.
   - Share a scripture with someone for encouragement.
   - Share with someone how Jesus has made a difference in your life.
   - Invite someone to church, Bible study or prayer meeting.
   - Share Christian music with someone
   - Share the Gospel of Jesus Christ with someone who needs to receive Him as Savior.

   When have you felt the leading and power of the Holy Spirit while taking any of these steps?

   _____
   _____

2. Which of these simple steps is your greatest area of strength and which is your greatest area of weakness?

   _____
   _____

   * Never be discouraged by areas of weakness. This is where Jesus promises to demonstrate His greatest power. Remember that God's Word tells us: *"My grace is sufficient for thee: for my strength is made perfect in weakness"* (2 Corinthians 12:9).

3. What other simple steps has the Holy Spirit shown you to take to be a witness for Christ to your world?

   _____
   _____
   _____

My Prayer from the Heart

Heavenly Father,

Your Word promises that I shall be a witness to the world around me. Baptize me with Your Spirit and Your power, so that I can speak to those You lead me to with words and deeds, and with wisdom and power.

In Jesus' name,

The Lord's Answer/s to Me

_____

_____

_____

_____

Day 4

Do You Know Him As Lord of the Harvest?

Pray ye therefore the Lord of the harvest, that he will send forth labourers into his harvest. Matthew 9:38

One evening, while praying with a friend, I had a vision of a field, and there was someone in that field. To me, this person looked like someone from Bible days. I asked the Lord what this meant. He told me, "I am the Lord of the Harvest, and I am in the midst of the harvest fields."

Jesus is Lord of the Harvest, and He's calling for more laborers to join Him in the harvest fields. He's calling you and me to this exalted privilege, to serve as His hands, His feet, His heart and His mouthpiece to those around us.

No matter what harvest field the Lord leads us to, He is with us—stirring our faith, giving us words and causing testimonies to come to our remembrance. We seem to be always fearful that we're not worthy to co-labor with Him in the fields, yet in the midst of the harvest fields, God's perfect love will cast out these fears. His love will drive out any concerns we might have of being rejected by those we approach, and He will give us the sensitivity to be the kind of light He needs us to be.

In the midst of the harvest fields of everyday life, God is drawing people unto Himself through the power of His Holy Spirit, and He is calling you and me into the harvest fields to join Him. Will you answer His call?

SCRIPTURE KEYS TO DECLARE

1 Peter 3:15:
But sanctify the Lord God in your hearts: and be ready always to give an answer to every man that asketh you a reason of the hope that is in you with meekness and fear.

Philippians 4:13:
I can do all things through Christ which strengtheth me.

Matthew 10:32:
Whosoever therefore shall confess me before men, him will I confess also before my Father which is in heaven.

Matthew 4:19:
And he [Jesus] saith unto them, follow me, and I will make you fishers of men.

Harvesting Souls

POINTS TO PONDER

Harvest Fields Galore!

1. Just as Jesus spoke to the woman at the well, He provides us with many opportunities to speak to those who need a Savior. Circle possible opportunities where you would be willing to join in faith with the Lord of the Harvest: Traveling on an airplane, waiting for an appointment, sitting at a bus stop, standing in the grocery store line, sharing coffee with a friend or speaking with a neighbor. List other possible ideas:

_____

_____

2. Jesus spent time with the sinners and tax collectors, seeking out the lost and giving them direction. Ask yourself: are you limiting all of your spare time to church activities? Set a goal to spend some time reaching out to people in your harvest fields. List your goals for reaching out:

_____

_____

3. Jesus sent out the disciples two by two. Think of one or more Christian friends who might commit with you to spend time being a witness. Ideas for you and your friends might include: Forming a parents' support group, visiting a nursing home, volunteering at a school or community agency, joining a team sport, visiting the sick at a hospital or reaching out to neighbors. What are YOUR ideas? And who will you ask to be a willing witness with you?

_____

_____

My Prayer from the Heart

Heavenly Father,

Show me people to whom I can reach out, and reveal to me other Christians who would be willing to join me in witnessing for You. Establish my priorities, so that my time and efforts will include spending time in Your harvest fields, sharing the Good News of salvation through Jesus Christ.

In Jesus' name,

The Lord's Answer/s to Me

Day 5

Preparing the Ground

Behold, a sower went forth to sow; and ... some ... fell into good ground, and brought forth fruit.   Matthew 13:3-4 and 8

God needs more *"labourers"* in His harvest fields, and an agricultural laborer does much more than simply harvest. First, of course, the ground must be plowed and planted before any harvest is possible. Once a farmer has plowed and then planted and cultivated his seed, still he must patiently await the expected harvest.

Christian laborers, just like earthly farmers, need to first plow the soil of the human heart with prayer, testimonies and demonstrations of the love of God. During this process, the Holy Spirit labors with us, softening the heart of the person, watering seeds planted by willing laborers and stirring faith into their heart.

The fact that we need plowing, seeding, cultivating and then harvesting reminds us to always seek the Lord to determine what type of ground we're sowing into. Touching a hardened heart requires much prayer (and sometimes fasting), much declaration of God's Word and the sensitivity to know what words and actions will help to soften it. Some hearts may have terribly stony places that must be removed before any seed can grow in them.

A heart that is ready and willing to receive Jesus as Lord and Savior represents a ready harvest. Ask the Lord for wisdom in the field. He will reveal to you the condition of every heart and what type of labor is needed to prepare it. Then, in faith, know that whatever labor is required, God reveals to us fields that are *"white already to harvest"* (John 4:35). See that harvest today in faith.

Scripture Keys to Declare

Genesis 8:22:
While the earth remaineth, seedtime and harvest ... shall not cease.

1 Corinthians 3:6-9:
I have planted, Apollos watered; but God gave the increase. So then neither is he that planteth any thing, neither he that watereth; but God that giveth the increase. Now he that planteth and he that watereth are one: and every man shall receive his own reward according to his own labour. For we are labourers together with God.

Mark 4:28-29:
For the earth bringeth forth fruit of herself; first the blade, then the ear, after that the full corn in the ear. But when the fruit is brought forth, immediately he putteth in the sickle, because the harvest is come.

Harvesting Souls

Points to Ponder

Knowing the Ground of Your Harvest Fields

1. In your list of harvest fields (people you know), which ones represent hard ground? Stony ground? Who is softening toward the Lord?

   _____
   _____

2. Dealing with hard ground requires the heavenly tools of Christlike behavior. Circle the behaviors you currently exercise for your harvest fields:
   - Prayer
   - Fasting
   - Forgiveness
   - Helping others
   - Declaring God's Word
   - Unconditional love

   List other heavenly tools you can think of:

   _____
   _____

3. Think of those who demonstrate hearts that are softening toward the Lord Jesus and consider: What are you doing to bring them closer to salvation?
   - Invite them to church or Christian fellowship.
   - Pray with them and/or share scriptures.
   - Share a Christian tape, book or CD.
   - Explain how Jesus has made a difference in your life.

     List other ideas:

   _____
   _____
   _____

My Prayer from the Heart

Heavenly Father,

Help me to understand the condition of the hearts in my harvest fields. Help me to sow seeds and willingly labor in those fields. Help me to know that You are already sending out Your angels to reap the harvest. Give me faith to know that my labors will make a difference in the harvest of souls.

In Jesus' name,

The Lord's Answer/s to Me

Day 6

An Overcoming Witness

And they overcame him by the blood of the Lamb, and by the word of their testimony; and they loved not their lives unto the death.   Revelation 12:11

One of the most effective tools we have to defeat Satan and his powers of darkness is our witness for Christ. Anytime we testify of ways that Jesus has brought victory to our lives, we impart a portion of that overcoming power to others. For example, if I talk to someone who is struggling with alcohol or drugs, I can testify to them that the power of Jesus Christ delivered some of my own family members from these very addictions. And regardless of the reaction of those to whom I testify, I've still planted a seed of faith in them about the overcoming power of our Lord.

People need hope, they need faith, and they need to be told that Jesus Christ is *"the way, the truth, and the life"* for their particular circumstances (John 14:6). Stir up the faith within you and begin to share your overcoming witness with those you encounter in your daily life.

SCRIPTURE KEYS TO DECLARE

Revelation 12:10-11:
And I heard a loud voice saying in heaven, Now is come salvation, and strength, and the kingdom of our God, and the power of his Christ: for the accuser of our brethren is cast down, which accused them before our God day and night. And they overcame him by the blood of the Lamb, and by the word of their testimony; and they loved not their lives unto the death.

2 Timothy 1:6-8:
Wherefore I put thee in remembrance that thou stir up the gift of God, which is in thee by the putting on of my hands. For God hath not given us the spirit of fear; but of power, and of love, and of a sound mind. Be not thou therefore ashamed of the testimony of our Lord.

Harvesting Souls

POINTS TO PONDER

Your Overcoming Witness

1. The Word of God instructs us to be ready to share our testimony with others because the power to overcome is found in the blood of the Lamb (Jesus) and the word of our testimony. What are some testimonies you can share with others? Did Jesus bring you joy? Did He deliver you from any serious problems? Has He simply been your faithful Savior? List at least three ways that you can testify about His goodness to others:

_____
_____
_____

2. To whom have you witnessed about Christ? What was their response?

_____
_____
_____

3. Think of your harvest fields (the people you know). Considering this group of people, what are some testimonies you might share that could lead them closer to Jesus?

_____
_____
_____

Awakening to the Heartbeat of God

My Prayer from the Heart

Heavenly Father,

Stir my heart to remember how You have made a difference in my life. Prepare the hearts in my harvest fields, as I willingly testify to them about You. In faith, I know that the blood of Jesus and the words of my testimony will bring power to defeat the enemy in other people's lives, just as they have in my own.

In Jesus' name,

The Lord's Answer/s to Me

_____

_____

_____

_____

Day 7

The Gospel in a Nutshell

God is love. In this was manifested the love of God toward us, because that God sent his only begotten Son into the world, that we might live through him. 1 John 4:8-9

There are many tools for sharing the Gospel, such as tracts, tapes and videos. I once used a toy nutshell. This nutshell contained a pullout multicolored ribbon, representing God's Word about Jesus and His love for us. Each color had an important significance that we could then share:

GOLD reminds us of God's love. He *"is love"* (1 John 4:8). Gold also reminds us of the heavenly realm and the glory of God. BLACK represents the fact that sin separates us from God's love and prevents us from receiving His love. Paul wrote to the Romans, *"For all have sinned, and come short of the glory of God"* (Romans 3:23). RED represents the blood of Jesus and the fact that He died for our sins. *"For God so loved the world, that he gave his only begotten Son, that whosoever believeth in him should not perish, but have everlasting life"* (John 3:16). Jesus represents the gift of God's forgiveness and the opportunity to live a life in fellowship with God the Father. WHITE represents the fact that God will wash away our sins once we make a commitment to repent of (or turn away from) our sins and receive Jesus as our personal Lord and Savior. A true, heart-led desire to receive Jesus results in being born again into God's Kingdom. Jesus said, *"Verily, verily, I say unto thee, except a man be born again, he cannot see the kingdom of God"* (John 3:3). Paul declared: *"Whosoever shall call upon the name of the Lord shall be saved"* (Romans 10:13) and *"If thou shalt confess with thy mouth the Lord Jesus, and shalt believe in thine heart that God hath raised him from the dead, thou shalt be saved"* (Romans 10:9).

Now, what is significant about the nutshell? It represents a hardened heart, without Jesus. The Gospel scriptures, when sowed into a heart and watered, become the nutcracker. The power of the Gospel can crack open even the hardest of hearts.

SCRIPTURE KEYS TO DECLARE

1 Corinthians 1:18:
For the preaching of the cross is to them that perish foolishness; but unto us which are saved it is the power of God.

John 5:24:
Verily, verily, I say unto you, he that heareth my word, and believeth on him that sent me, hath everlasting life, and shall not come into condemnation; but is passed from death unto life.

1 John 4:15:
Whosoever shall confess that Jesus is the Son of God, God dwelleth in him, and he in God.

Harvesting Souls

POINTS TO PONDER

Sowing Gospel Seeds

1. What methods have you used to share the Gospel with others?
   - None yet
   - Books
   - Tracts
   - Videos, Christian music
   - Sharing the Gospel
   - Evangelism teams

   _____
   _____
   _____
   _____

2. Whom do you know who might be able to disciple you, so that you, in turn, can more easily and effectively share the Gospel?

   _____
   _____
   _____
   _____

3. Think of the main themes for presenting the Lord Jesus through God's Word. Look up scriptures that represent the following themes:
   - God's love
   - Repentance
   - Jesus as our Savior
   - Receiving Jesus

   _____
   _____
   _____

Awakening to the Heartbeat of God

My Prayer from the Heart

Heavenly Father,

I want to use the Gospel of Jesus Christ just as a nutcracker is used to open a hard shell. Show me ways to share scripture keys for salvation in my harvest fields. Equip me with encouragers, books, music and revelation knowledge of Your Word. I trust You to teach me—even as You prepare the hearts with whom I will share Your Gospel, trusting that it has power to bring forth salvation!

In Jesus' name,

The Lord's Answer/s to Me

_____

_____

_____

_____

Day 8

Sad Heart, Happy Heart

A new heart also will I give you, and a new spirit will I put within you: and I will take away the stony heart out of your flesh, and I will give you an heart of flesh.
Ezekiel 36:26

Recently I saw a bumper sticker with a powerful witness for Jesus Christ. It simply showed a sad face and a happy face. The sad face had the caption "my life before Jesus," and the happy face simply said, "my life after Jesus." In this fast-paced world, those two simple lines get right to the point. For anyone who gets overwhelmed with sharing the Gospel, try this simple, but very effective method. Better yet: how about just saying "sad heart, happy heart."

First, draw a heart with a sad face inside of it. Explain to the person you show it to that when our choices in life don't line up with God's Word, and when we don't give Jesus the opportunity to live in our hearts, the result is a sad heart—for us, for Him and for others. Why is this sad for Jesus? Because He wants to live in our hearts, to bring us joy, peace and righteous choices through His power. He died for this privilege, and it's sad when anyone rejects Him.

Next draw a heart with a happy face inside of it. Explain to the person you show it to that they need to give control of their lives and hearts to Jesus and that the result will be a new heart, one filled with God's love, a happy heart. That's what it means to be born anew into the Kingdom of God!

Sad Heart
No Jesus!

Happy Heart
With Jesus!

SCRIPTURE KEYS TO DECLARE

Psalm 51:10:
Create in me a clean heart, O God; and renew a right spirit within me.

Romans 14:17:
For the kingdom of God is not meat and drink; but righteousness, and peace, and joy in the Holy Ghost.

2 Corinthians 5:17:
Therefore if any man be in Christ, he is a new creature: old things are passed away; behold, all things are become new.

Harvesting Souls

POINTS TO PONDER

Talking About the Hearts

1. Draw a heart with a sad face inside of it. List the choices you made in life that resulted in sadness and negative results. (For example: worry, stress, stealing, addictions or unforgiveness.) How did these choices cause sadness for others?

   _____
   _____
   _____

2. Now draw a heart with a smiling face inside of it. What were the positive results from asking Jesus into your heart? Who else has had joy as a result of your life with Jesus?

   _____
   _____
   _____

3. Now, share this simple method of witness with someone. What were the results from this simple witness?

   _____
   _____

   * Remember, whatever the immediate results, God faithfully waters the seed, and it will eventually bring forth fruit!

Awakening to the Heartbeat of God

My Prayer from the Heart

Heavenly Father,

Help me to always treasure and walk in the joy of my salvation. Help me to be quick to witness to others that You are ready to replace their human heart with Your heart, complete with righteousness, peace and joy. Prepare the hearts in my harvest field!

In Jesus' name,

THE LORD'S ANSWER/S TO ME

_____

_____

_____

_____

Day 9

Taking a Walk on the Roman Road

For whosoever shall call upon the name of the Lord shall be saved.   Romans 10:13

    A popular tract used for witnessing has often been called "The Roman Road" because it outlines God's plan of salvation from the book of Romans. Without using the tract, you can mark the pertinent verses in your Bible and then simply read each one out loud as you witness. They are: Romans 3:23, Romans 6:23, Romans 10:13 and Romans 10:9-10.

    Step 1: Explain that God loves us and He wants us to experience His love and His glory! **Step 2**: Read Romans 3:23 (*"For all have sinned, and come short of the glory of God"*) and explain that we all fall short of God's glory. You might want to tell some ways that you've fallen short in your own life and to ask the people you're witnessing to if they've ever fallen short in theirs**.** **Step 3:** Read Romans 6:23 (*"For the wages of sin is death; but the gift of God is eternal life through Jesus Christ our Lord"*). Explain that according to God's Word, the wages (or payment) for our sins is *"death"* but that God has provided us with a gift that we can choose instead of continuing to suffer the consequences of sin. That gift is Jesus Christ. It's not enough, though, to know that He is our gift for eternal life; we need to take another step and allow Him to become our Lord! **Step 4:** Read Romans 10:13 (as stated above). Explain that the next step is to call on the

Awakening to the Heartbeat of God

name of the Lord Jesus Christ, as a personal source of forgiveness. "Then," tell the person, "you will be saved." Offer to pray with them if they're ready for this step. A simple, heartfelt prayer at this moment might be something like this: "Jesus, I know that I have sinned, and I ask for Your forgiveness. Come into my heart and be my Lord and Savior." Then take Step 5: Read Romans 10:9-10 (*"That if thou shalt confess with thy mouth the Lord Jesus, and shalt believe in thine heart that God hath raised him from the dead, thou shalt be saved. For with the heart man believeth unto righteousness; and with the mouth confession is made unto salvation"*) and then ask them to repeat this promise. Encourage them to confess Jesus as Lord and Savior. If they do, next have them touch their own heart and remind them that Jesus has now been given a new home in a new heart!

SCRIPTURE KEYS TO DECLARE

Romans 10:12:
For there is no difference between the Jew and the Greek: for the same Lord over all is rich unto all that call upon him.

Romans 10:14-15:
How then shall they call on him in whom they have not believed? And how shall they believe in him of whom they have not heard? And how shall they hear without a preacher? And how shall they preach, except they be sent? As it is written, How beautiful are the feet of them that preach the gospel of peace, and bring glad tidings of good things!

Romans 10:17:
So then faith cometh by hearing, and hearing by the word of God.

Harvesting Souls

POINTS TO PONDER

Walking Along the Roman Road

1. In the margin next to Romans 3:23 in your Bible, write the next verse, "Romans 6:23." Next to Romans 6:23, record "Romans 10:13." Next to Romans 10:13, include "Romans 10:9-10." These references will give you the consecutive steps for walking along the Roman Road. Did you do it? Yes _____ No _____

2. Now, it's time to practice. Open your Bible to Romans 3:23, read the scripture and trust the Holy Spirit to help you explain it in your own words. Did you do it? Yes _____ No _____

3. Practice with one or more Christian friends. List those with whom you practice and the results.
   _____
   _____

4. Finally, it's time to seek the Lord and ask Him to show you someone in your harvest field who may be willing to hear about the Roman Road. As you are planting seeds, be sensitive to whether or not the person is a ready harvest, willing to accept Jesus! Afterward, list your results:
   _____
   _____
   _____

Awakening to the Heartbeat of God

My Prayer from the Heart

Heavenly Father,

Prepare the hearts of those to whom I will speak. For my Christian friends, stir evangelism in their hearts, as I practice sharing Your Word with them. And, for the harvest field, prepare those who will be willing to receive Your Word and then receive You as Lord and Savior.

In Jesus' name,

The Lord's Answer/s to Me

_____

_____

_____

_____

Day 10

What Will You Give Up to See Captives Set Free?

The spirit of the Lord is upon me, because he hath anointed me to preach the gospel to the poor; he hath sent me to heal the brokenhearted, to preach deliverance to the captives, and recovering of sight to the blind, to set at liberty them that are bruised, to preach the acceptable year of the Lord.   Luke 4:18-19

This is how Jesus began His ministry. He was willing to give everything to see captives set free. He gave His time, His prayers, His friendship and His strength. In the end, He allowed His very life to be sacrificed so that we may experience forgiveness and fellowship with our heavenly Father.

How about you? What are you willing to give up to see captives set free? Will you give of your time, your talents and your resources to encourage and disciple those who need to have their eyes opened to God's Word? Are you praying for people to have ears to hear the Gospel and a heart to receive it? Would you fast (food, television, etc.) and pray *"to loose the bands of wickedness, to undo the heavy burdens, and to let the oppressed go free"* (Isaiah 58:6)?

Awakening to the Heartbeat of God

Seek the Lord and ask Him to prioritize your life. Ask Him to show you how you can be used by Him to bring the Gospel to the poor and deliverance to the captives.

SCRIPTURE KEYS TO DECLARE

Isaiah 58:6-12:
Is not this the fast that I have chosen? To loose the bands of wickedness, to undo the heavy burdens, and to let the oppressed go free, and that ye break every yoke? Is it not to deal thy bread to the hungry, and that thou bring the poor that are cast out to thy house? When thou seest the naked, that thou cover him; and that thou hide not thyself from thine own flesh? Then shall thy light break forth as the morning, and thine health shall spring forth speedily: and thy righteousness shall go before thee; the glory of the Lord shall be thy rereward. Then shalt thou call, and the Lord shall answer; thou shalt cry, and he shall say, Here I am. If thou take away from the midst of thee the yoke, the putting forth of the finger, and speaking vanity; and if thou draw out thy soul to the hungry, and satisfy the afflicted soul; then shall thy light rise in obscurity, and thy darkness be as the noon day: and the Lord shall guide thee continually, and satisfy thy soul in drought, and make fat thy bones: and thou shalt be like a watered garden, and like a spring of water, whose waters fail not. And they that shall be of thee shall build the old waste places: thou shalt raise up the foundations of many generations; and thou shalt be called, The repairer of the breach, The restorer of paths to dwell in.

Harvesting Souls

POINTS TO PONDER

What Will You Give Up?

1. Read aloud Luke 4:18-19. In what ways do you help preach the Gospel to the poor?
   _____
   _____
   _____

2. To whom can Jesus send you who needs healing for a broken heart? Ask the Lord to show you how to encourage others to seek His healing touch. What did He tell you?
   _____
   _____
   _____

3. Ask the Lord about an individual fast (a meal, a favorite television program or whatever other type of fast the Lord speaks to your heart to do). During the time you're fasting, specifically pray for your harvest fields. Pray for their deliverance and recovery of sight and for spiritual liberty in their lives. List what the Lord shows you to do, and then follow through with obedience:
   _____
   _____
   _____
   _____

4. Give the Lord your priorities, time and talents. List ways in which He shows you that you can give of yourself for your harvest fields.
   _____
   _____
   _____

Awakening to the Heartbeat of God

My Prayer from the Heart

Heavenly Father,

Your Word tells me to take up my cross and follow You. Help me lay down *my* priorities and seek Yours. Help me to follow You into the harvest fields. Strengthen me to fast and pray for the Gospel of Christ to be received by the people in my harvest fields. With Your eyes, I choose to see the captives set free!

In Jesus' name,

The Lord's Answer/s to Me

_____

_____

_____

_____

Day 11

Hospitality, Jesus' Style

But their scribes and Pharisees murmured against his disciples, saying, Why do ye eat and drink with publicans and sinners? And Jesus answering said unto them, They that are whole need not a physician; but they that are sick. I came not to call the righteous, but sinners to repentance.

Luke 5:30-32

Jesus was never concerned about being in the popular circles. Rather, He spent time with those to whom His heavenly Father sent Him. From early childhood, He was always about His Father's business (see Luke 2:49). The scribes and the Pharisees were quick to criticize Him because of this, yet He was also quick to answer them. He had not come to pass His time with the righteous; it was the sinners who needed Him.

We, too, must spend time with those who need the Lord. For this reason, the Lord gives us the gift of hospitality. Inviting people into Christian fellowship helps further God's Kingdom in two ways: (1) It helps build up the Body of Christ, and (2) It helps draw a needy world to God's love. Be careful that your social time has God's purposes in mind. Listen to the Holy Spirit as He reveals to you those He wants you to reach out to. As you show them God's love, they will become more open to receive Jesus into their lives.

Scripture Keys to Declare

Hebrews 13:2:
Be not forgetful to entertain strangers.

Luke 14:12-14:
When thou makest a dinner or a supper, call not thy friends, nor thy brethren, neither thy kinsmen, nor thy rich neighbours; lest they also bid thee again, and a recompense be made thee. But when thou makest a feast, call the poor, the maimed, the lame, the blind. And thou shalt be blessed; for they cannot recompense thee; for thou shall be recompensed at the resurrection of the just.

Luke 15:1-7:
Then drew near unto him all the publicans and sinners for to hear him. And the Pharisees and scribes murmured, saying, This man receiveth sinners, and eateth with them. And he spake this parable unto them, saying, What man of you, having an hundred sheep, if he lose one of them, doth not leave the ninety and nine in the wilderness, and go after that which is lost, until he find it? And when he hath found it, he layeth it on his shoulders, rejoicing. And when he cometh home, he calleth together his friends and neighbours, saying unto them, rejoice with me; for I have found my sheep which was lost. I say unto you, that likewise joy shall be in heaven over one sinner that repenteth, more than over ninety and nine just persons, which need no repentance.

Harvesting Souls

POINTS TO PONDER

How Do You Show Hospitality?

1. Here are some ways to show hospitality to others. Circle the methods you've used. Reach out in kindness to someone new in church, invite friends, neighbors or co-workers to a church fellowship, spend time, as the Lord leads, with someone in need of Christian fellowship, have a pot luck meal and invite a combination of Christian friends and others who need to be drawn into Christian fellowship. List other ideas the Lord shows you:

_____
_____
_____

2. Do you tend to spend time with the same circle of friends or the same people at church? List some ways the Lord shows you to extend hospitality to others:

_____
_____
_____

3. Here are some simple ways to show hospitality without taking too much time. Circle ideas to consider: Give a card of encouragement to someone, make a fruit basket (or other type of basket) for someone who needs to be blessed and encouraged, take time to listen to people in your daily life (offer to pray for them, if that opportunity arises), give an encouraging Christian book, tape, or video to someone who needs it.

    List other ideas:

_____
_____
_____

Awakening to the Heartbeat of God

My Prayer from the Heart

Heavenly Father,

You spent time with the sinners, strangers and the sick, as well as with Your disciples. You never allowed religious thinking to keep You from reaching out to the lost. Help me to spend time both in Christian fellowship and in reaching out to a needy world. Give me eyes to see those who are hungry and thirsty for You and wisdom to release to You those who are not ready to receive. In all ways, help my times of fellowship to have Kingdom purposes.

In Jesus' name,

The Lord's Answer/s to Me

Day 12

Prayer Evangelism

Drop down [rain down], ye heavens, from above, and let the skies pour down righteousness: let the earth open, and let them bring forth salvation, and let righteousness spring up together.   Isaiah 45:8

Many have learned the scriptural principle: one man plants, another man waters, but God gives the increase (see 1 Corinthians 3:6). Prayer is a necessary part of this process. Prayer stirs faith into our lives to plant the seeds of Christian witness into our harvest fields. It also causes the Holy Spirit to rain down upon seeds already sown into our harvest fields—seeds of kind deeds, Christian fellowship, ministering to people's needs and simply allowing the love of Jesus to soften the hearts of those around us. The result is that salvation is brought forth and righteousness springs up.

Think about the field of people Jesus is telling you to pray for. Then let your prayers rise up to Heaven on their behalf. You can be assured that you will experience the rain of the Holy Spirit, as our heavenly Father brings you the desired results. Just as rain prepares a natural field for harvest, your prayer brings forth the conditions needed for your field to be harvested. Hear the Lord's call: *"The harvest is come"* (Mark 4:29).

Scripture Keys to Declare

Isaiah 43:5-8:
Fear not: for I am with thee: I will bring thy seed from the east, and gather thee from the west; I will say to the north, give up; and to the south, keep not back: bring my sons from far, and my daughters from the ends of the earth; even every one that is called by my name: for I have created him for my glory, I have formed him; yea, I have made him. Bring forth the blind people that have eyes, and the deaf that have ears.

Luke 3:6:
And all flesh shall see the salvation of God.

James 5:16:
The effectual fervent prayer of a righteous man availeth much.

James 5:20:
He which converteth the sinner from the error of his way, shall save a soul from death, and shall hide a multitude of sins.

Joshua 1:3:
Every place that the sole of your foot shall tread upon, that have I given unto you.

Harvesting Souls

POINTS TO PONDER

Saturate Your Fields with Prayer

1. Read Ephesians 3:4-20. Here God's Word states that it is His will for Christ to dwell in our hearts by faith and that we be rooted and grounded in His love. Look again at the list of people in your harvest fields and declare Ephesians 3:4-20 on their behalf. Did you do it? Yes ____ No ____

2. Read Joshua 1:3. Every place that the sole of our feet treads upon God intends to make a part of His Kingdom. Read through this list of possible areas of harvest fields to pray and walk through, declaring salvation as you do so: Your neighborhood, a local school ground, church buildings (believe for the harvest to come to every church in your area) and community centers. List others that you think of:
_____
_____
_____
_____

3. Now choose one or more prayer partners and follow through on some prayer walking. List where you prayed:
_____
_____
_____
_____

4. Read 1 John 1:7. God's Word tells us that the blood of Jesus Christ, His Son, cleanses us from all sin. Declare the blood of Jesus upon your harvest fields. As you declare this, know that His blood was shed to bring salvation to these very fields. Did you do it? Yes ____ No ____

My Prayer from the Heart

Heavenly Father,

Show me how to pray for my personal harvest fields. Show me where to walk, declaring that the blood of Jesus Christ brings forth the salvation of souls. Cause me to see the rain of your Holy Spirit and the harvest ready to come forth.

In Jesus' name,

The Lord's Answer/s to Me

_____

_____

_____

_____

Day 13

A Harvest Requires Light

Then spake Jesus again unto them, saying, I am the light of the world: he that followeth me shall not walk in darkness, but shall have the light of life.   John 8:12

A long time ago I learned of three things plants need in order to grow and produce: air, water and light. What would happen if you planted seeds of corn into quality soil and provided them with air and water, but then you kept the plants in a dark shed, denying them life-giving light. The result, of course, would be a total lack of harvest.

With a spiritual harvest (a soul birthed into God's Kingdom), the three essentials are the same. Air is needed (the breath of God upon our harvest fields by the power of His Holy Spirit). The water, representing the Word of God being established in people's hearts, is also vital. And what is the light? Jesus is *"the light of the world"* and He has promised that those who follow Him shall *"not walk in darkness,"* but shall have *"the light of life."*

So where do you and I fit into all this? We are called to be carriers of Jesus Christ, shining His life-giving light into the harvest fields around us. He said: *"Let your light so shine before men, that they may see your good works, and glorify your Father which is in Heaven"* (Matthew 5:16). What happens when we bring enough light into the field of someone's life? God's Word declares: *"For God, who commanded the light to shine out of darkness, hath shined in our hearts, to give the light of the knowledge of the glory of God in the face of Jesus Christ"* (2 Corinthians 4:6). It's time to allow some of the bright shining light from our churches to be carried into some of the dark areas of our world, places in desperate need of light. Will you be a carrier of that light?

SCRIPTURE KEYS TO DECLARE

2 Corinthians 4:3:
But if our gospel be hid, it is hid to them that are lost: in whom the God of this world hath blinded the minds of them which believe not, lest the light of the glorious gospel of Christ, who is the image of God, should shine unto them.

Psalm 119:105:
Thy word is a lamp unto my feet, and a light unto my path.

John 12:35-36:
Yet a little while is the light with you. Walk while ye have the light, lest darkness come upon you: for he that walketh in darkness knoweth not whither he goeth. While ye have light, believe in the light, that ye may be the children of light.

Acts 26:18:
To open their eyes, and to turn them from darkness to light, and from the power of Satan unto God, that they may receive forgiveness of sins, and inheritance among them which are sanctified by faith that is in me [Jesus].

Harvesting Souls

POINTS TO PONDER

Where Are You Shining Your Light?

1. List the places (other than church and Christian fellowship) where you let the light of Jesus shine through you:
   _____
   _____
   _____

2. Read the story of the Good Samaritan in Luke 10:30-37 and then list some occasions in which you have served the Lord as the Good Samaritan did.
   _____
   _____

3. Think of times when you were too busy to do the right thing, just like the religious leaders in the story of the Good Samaritan. Ask Jesus, your Shepherd, to show you His priorities for your life. List them here:
   _____
   _____
   _____

4. Here are some ways that we shine light into a dark world. Circle the ways in which you have been a light:
   - Smiling
   - Sharing Christian music
   - Kind deeds
   - Graciousness
   - Forgiveness
   - Christlike love

   List other ways in which you have been a light:
   _____
   _____
   _____

My Prayer from the Heart

Heavenly Father,

Let me be a carrier of light, shining a path for a needy world. Let me be exactly like the path of the just, *"as the shining light, that shineth more and more"* for the world to see (Proverbs 4: 18). Forgive me for those times when I have hidden my light. Stir the fire of my heart to be a source of warmth and light for a cold, dark world.

In Jesus' name,

The Lord's Answer/s to Me

_____

_____

_____

_____

Day 14

Prepare Their Hearts, Lord, with Our Words

Finally, brethren, whatsoever things are true, whatsoever things are honest, whatsoever things are just, whatsoever things are pure, whatsoever things are lovely, whatsoever things are of a good report; if there be any virtue, and if there be any praise, think on these things.
Philippians 4:8

Our words can make a difference in softening the hearts of those around us and preparing them to receive Christ. The words we speak and the attitude we demonstrate can warm the soil of a human heart.

Are your words full of praise to God? Do you speak words of appreciation to others? Do your conversations sow seeds of peace and unity, or do they sow strife and division? Is your day filled with joyful song, or is it more like the off-key drone of constant complaint and negativism? Consider Paul's words in Philippians 4:8.

As we consider these scriptures, let us be motivated to choose words that reflect Christlike character. As our words and attitudes shine with the love of Jesus, we will see the hearts of those in our harvest fields begin to blossom!

SCRIPTURE KEYS TO DECLARE

Proverbs 15:4:
A wholesome tongue is a tree of life.

Proverbs 15:7:
The lips of the wise disperse knowledge.

Proverbs 15:15:
All the days of the afflicted are evil: but he that is of a merry heart hath a continual feast.

Proverbs 18:21:
Death and life are in the power of the tongue: and they that love it shall eat the fruit thereof.

Harvesting Souls

POINTS TO PONDER

Submitting Our Tongues to God's Control

1. Read James 3:3-8, and then ask yourself: are your words filled with blessing or cursing? If your answer is not good, submit your tongue to Jesus today and allow the Holy Spirit to take control of your words.

   _____

   _____

2. James 1:19 tells us to be *"swift to hear, slow to speak, slow to wrath."* When anger is knocking at the door of your heart, are you quick to give control to the Holy Spirit? List some times when you allowed the Holy Spirit to keep you from speaking angry words.

   _____

   _____

   _____

3. Look at the following lines of behavior, and mark the ones you usually display. Then, ask the Holy Spirit to take more control of you in the areas that need more fruit of the Spirit.

The Fruit of the Flesh	The Fruit of the Spirit
Gossip	Confidentiality
Words of division	Words of unity
Criticism	Praise
Complaint	Enthusiasm
Words of hatred and anger	Words of love and peace
Words of doubt	Words of faith
Bitterness and unforgiveness	Understanding and forgiveness

My Prayer from the Heart

Heavenly Father,

Help me to understand how my words and my display of attitude can affect the people in my life. Help me to submit my tongue to You, allowing the Holy Spirit to take control of it. Help me to pray Your Word on behalf of the harvest fields around me. Even more importantly, help me to speak faith-filled words of love and kindness when I am in those harvest fields. Help my words to bring sunshine to the hearts of all the people in my life.

In Jesus' name,

The Lord's Answer/s to Me

_____

_____

_____

_____

Day 15

"But I Don't Like Persecution"

Father, forgive them; for they know not what they do.
Luke 23:34

Sometimes our witness for the Lord Jesus will cause people in our harvest fields to mistreat us. Their mistreatment represents the dreaded word that most Christians desperately want to avoid: persecution. Have you ever suffered persecution due to your witness for Jesus? Were you rejected, belittled or mocked? Were you a victim of gossip or mistreatment? Were you excluded, isolated from other people or judged for your beliefs? There's always a risk involved with being a witness for Christ, yet we must allow ourselves to become vulnerable for the sake of His Kingdom and for the good of lost souls.

Did you perhaps mistreat others who took risks with you? I can remember that as a young adult I was not kind to those who shared Jesus with me, and that included my own mother. And what was her response? She prayed for me, she loved me, she forgave me, and then she prayed for me some more.

I thank God for each and every person who risked persecution from me as they allowed the love of Jesus Christ to shine through them. I thank God for His only

Son, Jesus, who was beaten, spit upon, mocked and totally forsaken, and yet, He continued to love those who persecuted Him. He loved them so much that He prayed for their forgiveness. He endured all *"for the joy that was set before him"* (Hebrews 12:2).

No matter how you are treated in your harvest fields, allow our heavenly Father to stir forgiveness, refreshing and joy into your heart. The joy set before us will be souls!

SCRIPTURE KEYS TO DECLARE

Matthew 5:10-12:
Blessed are they which are persecuted for righteousness sake: for theirs is the kingdom of heaven. Blessed are ye, when men shall revile you, and persecute you, and shall say all manner of evil against you falsely, for my sake. Rejoice, and be exceedingly glad: for great is your reward in heaven: for so persecuted they the prophets which were before you.

Matthew 5:14:
Ye are the light of the world. A city that is set on an hill cannot be hid.

Matthew 5:44:
But I say unto you, love your enemies, bless them that curse you, do good to them that hate you, and pray for them which despitefully use you, and persecute you.

Harvesting Souls

POINTS TO PONDER

Growing through Persecution

1. Read Hebrews 11:33-40, and then list the types of persecution mentioned in these scriptures. What type of persecution do you experience here in your life?

   _____

   _____

2. List a few examples of times when people responded to your witness for Jesus in an unkind way.

   _____

   _____

3. Here are some Christlike responses for mistreatment. Circle the ones you have displayed: Forgiveness, blessing, patience, unconditional love and words of kindness. List others you think of:

   _____

   _____

   _____

4. One of the most common hindrances to sharing the love of Jesus is fear. God's Word tells us, in 2 Timothy 1:7, *"For God hath not given us the spirit of fear; but of power, and of love, and of a sound mind."* Ask the Holy Spirit to show you areas where you've been afraid to be a witness. List them here. Then ask Jesus to remove those fears, replacing them with His perfect love.

   _____

   _____

   _____

Awakening to the Heartbeat of God

My Prayer from the Heart

Heavenly Father,

Forgive me for times that I have not been a witness for You because I didn't want to be mistreated. Bless me with faith, love and a willingness to shine my witness for You into my personal harvest fields—no matter what the reaction of others may be. Help me to know that every seed of witness brings people closer to salvation.

In Jesus' name,

The Lord's Answer/s to Me

_____

_____

_____

_____

Day 16

Too Good Not to Share

O taste and see that the Lord is good: blessed is the man that trusteth in him.　　　　　　Psalm 34:8

One day my co-workers held a festive and delicious meal at our work place. It wasn't my birthday or any other special occasion, yet we find reasons to celebrate—especially when it comes to food. That day, they served one of my favorites: fruit smoothies made with fresh fruit and fruit juice blends. We had quite a variety to choose from: papaya, passion fruit, mango, strawberry, banana and the sweetest pineapple I had ever tasted. At the end of the day, one of my co-workers gave me a leftover pineapple to take home. It was sweet, ripe and ready to enjoy.

　　I took the pineapple home with me that evening, but I couldn't bring myself to eat it. Instead, I took it with me the next day and served it during morning break time to other co-workers in another clinic where I was working. The result was a group of smiling and thankful co-workers, all commenting that the pineapple I had brought was simply the sweetest they'd ever eaten. Somehow I knew that would be the reaction, and that's why I had saved the pineapple to share with them. That piece of fruit was just too good not to share.

Later that day, I was able to share some of my favorite bread with a co-worker, and then the Lord spoke to my heart. "My fruit is just too good not to share," He said, and I was reminded that His Word is bread and is also meant to be shared. When we think about the love of Jesus and all that He has done for us, isn't He just too good not to share?

So, are you ready? Break the bread, prepare the fruit and let us serve a needy world with the love and presence of our Lord Jesus Christ. And let us enjoy the experience of sharing.

SCRIPTURE KEYS TO DECLARE

John 21:17:
Jesus saith unto him, Feed my sheep.

Luke 4:18-19:
The Spirit of the Lord is upon me, because he hath anointed me to preach the gospel to the poor; he hath sent me to heal the brokenhearted, to preach deliverance to the captives, and recovering of sight to the blind, to set at liberty them that are bruised, to preach the acceptable year of the Lord.

John 15:8:
Herein is my Father glorified, that ye bear much fruit; so shall ye be my disciples.

Harvesting Souls

POINTS TO PONDER

Celebrating Jesus

1. Read Luke 15:7: *"I say unto you, that likewise joy shall be in heaven over one sinner that repenteth, more than over ninety and nine just persons, which need no repentance."* Close your eyes now, and think of the angels in Heaven rejoicing over each person who receives Jesus into their hearts. Doesn't that scene make you want to share His love more? Yes ___ No ___

2. List some of the testimonies that other people have shared with you which impacted your life:
   _____
   _____
   _____
   _____
   _____
   _____
   _____
   _____

3. List some testimonies that you can share with others, testimonies that will help them realize that Jesus is just too good not to share:
   _____
   _____
   _____
   _____

Awakening to the Heartbeat of God

My Prayer from the Heart

Heavenly Father,

Help me to share Your love in testimonies about Your faithfulness. Anoint my words to be nourishing and refreshing to the thirsty souls around me. Help my behavior to reflect the fruit of Your Spirit. Help me to also take time for Christlike fellowship and find opportunities to share Your Word, the bread of life, with hungry hearts.

In Jesus' name,

The Lord's Answer/s to Me

_____

_____

_____

_____

Part II

Dealing with Special Challenges

Day 17

"I'VE SINNED TOO MUCH TO BE SAVED"

For when we were yet without strength, in due time Christ died for the ungodly. ... But God commendeth his love toward us, in that, while we were yet sinners, Christ died for us.   Romans 5:6-8

Sometimes, when we witness to others about Christ, they may be hesitant to believe that they can be saved because they think they've sinned too much. This response is actually a cry of the human heart asking, "Is the love of Jesus deep enough to receive me?" This is a helpful scripture to remember in that moment.

Some of the greatest men and women of the Bible were examples of the great mercy of God visited upon sinners. King David, for instance, committed adultery and even murder, and yet God called him a man after His own heart. Why? It can only be explained by God's love and mercy.

The great apostle Paul called himself the chief of sinners, and his past also included killing innocent Christians. But he, too, learned that the love of Jesus is deep enough to receive even the vilest of sinners. He was able to mature into an apostle who knew the grace of God.

When someone you're witnessing to thinks they've sinned too much, tell them, "Your heavenly Father loves you too much to give up on you. Now, would you like to exchange your current life choices (and the resulting guilt and unworthiness) for God's gift of forgiveness, love and hope through Jesus Christ?" His love is wide enough to pour a sinful past into a sea of forgetfulness and deep enough to transform even the greatest of sinners into a righteous man or woman of God. No sin is too great for the outstretched arms of Jesus.

SCRIPTURE KEYS TO DECLARE

1 Timothy 1:15:
This is a faithful saying, and worthy of all acceptation, that Christ Jesus came into the world to save sinners; of whom I am chief.

Luke 19:10:
For the Son of man is come to seek and to save that which was lost.

John 6:37:
All that the Father giveth me shall come to me; and him that cometh to me I will in no wise cast out.

Harvesting Souls

POINTS TO PONDER

Seeds of Faith for the Challenge

1. List examples from your own life or the life of others in which the love of Jesus forgave and transformed. Such examples can then be used to encourage those to whom you witness.

_____
_____
_____
_____

2. Have you ever felt unworthy? List the ways in which the love and acceptance of Jesus ministered to you.

_____
_____
_____
_____

3. Here are some ways that we can show the love of Jesus to people who have felt unworthy: Give them a smile, a handshake or a hug (as the Lord leads), listen to them with acceptance, not judgment, share with them a meal or give to them an encouraging scripture. List other ideas that come to you:

_____
_____
_____
_____

My Prayer from the Heart

Heavenly Father,

The Bible declares to us that it's not the Father's will for any to perish, but for all to come to repentance. Help me to explain to others that if they're simply willing to confess their sins, You're faithful and just to forgive (1 John 1:9). Help me also to convince others that Your love is ready to be demonstrated to a heart that will simply call upon You. Help me to teach others about Your uncommon forgiveness, love and mercy.

In Jesus' name,

The Lord's Answer/s to Me

_____

_____

_____

_____

Day 18

"I'll Accept Christ 'Later'"

Behold, now is the accepted time; behold, now is the day of salvation.   2 Corinthians 6:2

Have you ever attempted to share your faith with someone, only to have them say that they *would* accept Jesus "later"? I can understand this attitude, and I know that it's a very serious mistake. It happened to me.

When I was still a teenager, one day I was invited to pray to receive Jesus as my Savior. I told the person that I wasn't ready just at that moment. This "later" mentality resulted in me making many foolish choices in life with negative consequences. I finally did ask Jesus to come into my heart, but not until I was about twenty-nine years old.

God says that *"NOW is the accepted time."* If you encounter a person who wants to put you off with this excuse, explain to them that we all have two choices. We can either open the door of our hearts to Jesus and His righteousness, peace and joy, or we open the door to our own reasoning and curiosity. Sadly, our human reasoning and curiosity tends to think that maybe life would be better without Christ.

Curiosity is like a Pandora's Box. In that tragic story, Pandora's curiosity caused her to open the mysterious box, and the result was not at all pleasant. Remind those to whom you witness that each day can bring life-filled choices and blessings through Jesus Christ or our own selfish choices can bring destruction and negative consequences. Appeal to their reasoning and curiosity by stating that life just might be better with Jesus. Next, stir their faith by declaring, "There is no doubt. Life *will* be better *with* Jesus. So, why not start today?"

SCRIPTURE KEYS TO DECLARE

Matthew 6:33:
But seek ye first the kingdom of God, and his righteousness; and all these things shall be added unto you.

Hebrews 3:15:
Today if ye will hear his voice, harden not your hearts.

Isaiah 55:6:
Seek ye the Lord while he may be found, call ye upon him while he is near.

Harvesting Souls

POINTS TO PONDER

Today Is the Day

1. Read Revelation 3:20: *"Behold, I stand at the door, and knock: if any man hear my voice, and open the door, I will come in to him, and will sup with him, and he with me."* Try this with someone to whom you witness. Ask them, "If I were knocking on your door today with a gift that promises to be a blessing for you forever, would you open the door?" Was the result positive? Yes ___ No ___

2. Here are examples of some things we tend to procrastinate with: getting up in the morning, cleaning the garage and working on a tedious project. Now isn't it true that we tend to feel better once we've followed through? Doesn't it tend to bring more order into our lives? Explain to those to whom you witness that when any of us follows through on accepting Jesus as Savior, it always brings more order into our lives. What was the result?

_____

_____

_____

3. Because today is the day for a sinner to be saved, it's also the day you need to share Jesus with someone who needs His love. Don't delay in sharing this, the most precious gift that anyone could ever receive. List some ideas of ways you can be a witness to people today.

_____

_____

_____

My Prayer from the Heart

Heavenly Father,

Help me to respond with wisdom to those who would seem to want to receive You "later." Let your Holy Spirit be present in those occasions, as I encourage others that choosing You today will bring righteousness, peace and joy-filled tomorrows.

In Jesus' name,

The Lord's Answer/s to Me

_____

_____

_____

_____

Day 19

"The Church Is Full of Hypocrites"

For the time is come that judgment must begin at the house of God: and if it first begin at us, what shall the end be of them that obey not the gospel of God?

1 Peter 4:17

Have you ever heard anyone use this excuse for not receiving Christ? I know this excuse well, for I used to also declare that the church was full of hypocrites ... that is, before I became a Christian. When I said this, those who were witnessing to me used a variety of tactics to overcome my objections.

One Christian used the strategy of Matthew 5:25: *"Agree with thine adversary quickly."* He agreed with me that the church contains hypocrites. After all, none of us is perfect. Then he apologized on behalf of the church for any Christians who may have hurt me.

Another Christian (my mom, this time) shattered this challenge by reminding me that it was the church that had fed her family when they didn't have enough food. Neither of these Christians argued with me, and their Christlike strategies paid off. Within a month, I started attending church.

A third strategy is to remind people that the Church is

filled with highly imperfect people, and yet we all love Jesus. Some of us have learned to love one another, while others are still learning. Then simply state that although Christians are not perfect, they are forgiven through Jesus Christ—the only perfect One.

SCRIPTURE KEYS TO DECLARE

Romans 14:12:
So then every one of us shall give account of himself to God.

1 John 3:3:
And every man that hath this hope in him purifieth himself, even as he is pure.*

1 John 5:5:
Who is he that overcometh the world, but he that believeth that Jesus is the Son of God?*

* These are important scriptures to remind people that Christians who love God are in an overcoming process, even now learning to purify themselves through Jesus Christ.

Harvesting Souls

POINTS TO PONDER

How Can You Deal with Hypocrisy?

1. Can you think of areas in your Christian life that may be viewed by others as hypocritical? Examples might include: gossiping, smoking, drinking, watching R-rated movies or inappropriate anger. Can you think of others?

_____
_____
_____

2. Ask our heavenly Father to shine His light upon your life, to forgive you for any lifestyle choices that may be a stumbling block to others and to help you change. He is a faithful change agent. Did you do it? Yes ___ No ___

3. What are some positive things that can be said about your church and its witness for Christlike character?

_____
_____
_____
_____

My Prayer from the Heart

Heavenly Father,

I don't want to be a stumbling block, preventing other people from receiving You as Lord and Savior. Help me to abide in You, walking daily by the power, might and wisdom of Your Spirit. Give me Christlike responses, in word and in deed, to any who have been hurt by hypocrisy in the Church. Please shine through me with Your righteousness, peace and joy. May my responses shatter the challenges and draw men and women closer to You.

In Jesus' name,

The Lord's Answer/s to Me

_____

_____

_____

_____

Day 20

"I Just Can't Change"

I can do all things through Christ which strengtheneth me.   Philippians 4:13

Sometimes people are afraid to receive Jesus because they think they won't be able to change their ways. They're afraid that they're too weak, with too many deeply ingrained bad habits. The goal with this type of challenge is to help people give their heart to Jesus, along with their fear of failure, in exchange for His supernatural, life-changing power.

It helps to explain that if we desire to change and live a better life, our Lord is faithful to transform our weaknesses and failures into strength and victory. God's Word promises that we *"can do all things through Christ."* It also gives us the right strategy—submit to God (through Jesus Christ), resist the devil, and *"he will flee"* (James 4:7). God's Word promises victory.

At this point, take the person's hand, and encourage him or her to submit to God by asking Jesus to forgive their sins and become their Lord and Savior. The power of Jesus will transform those I-can't-change challenges into fresh, new faith that, *"with God all things are possible"* (Matthew 19:26).

Scripture Keys to Declare

John 8:36:
If the Son therefore shall make you free, ye shall be free indeed.

1 John 5:4:
For whatsoever is born of God overcometh the world: and this is the victory that overcometh the world, even our faith.

2 Thessalonians 3:3:
But the Lord is faithful, who shall stablish you, and keep you from evil.

1 Corinthians 10:13:
There hath no temptation taken you but such as is common to man: but God is faithful, who will not suffer you to be tempted above that ye are able; but will with the temptation also make a way to escape, that ye may be able to bear it.

Harvesting Souls

POINTS TO PONDER

Building Strength for Change

1. Did you ever struggle with any ungodly behaviors? If so, how did the power of Jesus Christ help you change from those habits to more Christlike behavior?

   _____
   _____
   _____

2. List any current behaviors that you are now submitting to the Lord for change.

   _____
   _____
   _____

3. Think of how to share with others the many ways the power of Jesus has transformed your life. List your ideas:

   _____
   _____
   _____

4. Do you have any favorite scriptures that assure of the Lord's forgiveness? For instance, how did Jesus comfort *you* when *you* failed? Write them down:

   _____
   _____
   _____

My Prayer from the Heart

Heavenly Father,

Help me to encourage others to give You their fear of failure and to choose to trust You as Lord and Savior. Just as You have faithfully changed *me* from glory to glory, help me to encourage others that You will be faithful to change them too. Help me to assure them that You forgive, even when we fail, as long as we turn our failures over to You. Help me to teach others the promise of 1 John 1:9: *"If we confess our sins, he is faithful and just to forgive us our sins, and to cleanse us from all unrighteousness."*

In Jesus' name,

The Lord's Answer/s to Me

_____

_____

_____

_____

Day 21

"I'll Lose All My Friends"

He that loveth father or mother more than me is not worthy of me: and he that loveth son or daughter more than me is not worthy of me. And he that taketh not his cross, and followeth after me is not worthy of me. He that findeth his life shall lose it: and he that loseth his life for my sake shall find it. Matthew 10:37-39

For many people, the fear of losing friendships and close relationships can be a hindrance in asking Jesus into their heart. Friendships do change once someone chooses to live a life with Christ. A sincere, honest testimony of how Christianity affected your friendships would be a helpful strategy.

Another helpful answer would be to explain that our heavenly Father desires to give us relationships that will bless us and help us grow in our Christian faith. Asking Jesus into our hearts also results in greater wisdom. There will be less tendency to spend time with people who would encourage temptation and wrong choices.

I made the mistake, many years ago, of delaying a commitment to Jesus, choosing my friends over Him. This resulted in many years of difficult consequences. Encourage the people you witness to that Jesus is the best Friend they can ever hope to have. If they seek the Kingdom of God, through Jesus Christ, they can trust that God will do what is best for all their friendships. And He will also bless them with new friendships. Although relationships may shift and change through life, God will bring about His best through it all.

SCRIPTURE KEYS TO DECLARE

Proverbs 29:25:
*The fear of man bringeth a snare: but whoso putteth his trust in the L*ORD *shall be safe.*

Mark 8:36:
For what shall it profit a man, if he shall gain the whole world, and lose his own soul?

Proverbs 13:20:
He that walketh with wise men shall be wise: but a companion of fools shall be destroyed.

Harvesting Souls

POINTS TO PONDER

Let's Talk About Real Friendship

1. List the qualities of a good friend.

2. List the characteristics of friends with a negative influence.

3. List examples of how Jesus has been a Friend to you. Could you also explain this to someone you may witness to about Him?

4. How did knowing Jesus change the friendships and relationships in your life?

My Prayer from the Heart

Heavenly Father,

I know that a commitment to You can result in changed friendships and relationships. Give me wisdom and understanding to teach others that a relationship with You is worth risking possible changes in other relationships. Help me to explain to others the eternal, priceless worth of Your friendship.

In Jesus' name,

The Lord's Answer/s to Me

_____

_____

_____

_____

Day 22

"But I'm Not Living Right"

I am not come to call the righteous, but sinners to repentance. Matthew 9:13

Often, those we witness to will want to delay receiving Christ as Savior because they think they need to start living better *first*. The key is to help them understand that Jesus is their way to a better life. In fact, He is *"the way, the truth, and the life"* (John 14:6). No matter what type of life we have lived, our heavenly Father reaches out to us with arms of love, and He promises us a better life.

Think of the prodigal son. When he realized the mess his life had become, he stated: *"I will arise and go to my father, and will say unto him, Father, I have sinned against heaven and before thee"* (Luke 15:18). Did his father tell him to "clean up his act" first before he could love him? Of course not! Instead, when the prodigal son was yet a great way off, his father *"saw him, and had compassion, and ran, and fell on his neck, and kissed him"* (Luke 15:20). In the same way, our heavenly Father rejoices when anyone who has been experiencing a life dead with sin now chooses true life through Christ Jesus. He rejoices when someone who has been lost in the world is found through faith in Christ. Therefore, the answer for those who first want to become better people is to tell them to simply reach out to our heavenly Father. He has a robe to place upon them, a ring for their finger, and His Son, Jesus to transform their lives into something better.

Scripture Keys to Declare

Matthew 9:12-13:
They that be whole need not a physician, but they that are sick. But go ye and learn what that meaneth, I will have mercy, and not sacrifice: for I am not come to call the righteous, but sinners to repentance.

Ezekiel 36:26-27:
A new heart also will I give you, and a new spirit will I put within you: and I will take away the stony heart out of your flesh, and I will give you an heart of flesh. And I will put my spirit within you, and cause you to walk in my statutes, and ye shall keep my judgments, and do them.

Luke 19:10:
For the Son of man is come to seek and to save that which was lost.

Isaiah 44:22:
I have blotted out, as a thick cloud, thy transgressions, and, as a cloud, thy sins: return unto me; for I have redeemed thee.

Harvesting Souls

POINTS TO PONDER

Right Living? Or Righteousness with Jesus?

1. One of the reasons people may not feel ready to receive Jesus as Lord is that they're still drinking, smoking, watching ungodly movies or listening to ungodly music. List other reasons:

_____
_____
_____
_____

2. What testimonies could you share with others? What areas of your life was Jesus faithful to change?

_____
_____
_____
_____

3. Explain why your life has been easier to clean up *with* Jesus as compared to a life without Him.

_____
_____
_____
_____

My Prayer from the Heart

Heavenly Father,

Help me to understand that a person's heart under conviction may battle strong feelings of unworthiness. Give me wisdom to explain that our heavenly Father's love reaches out to them right where they are. Your power and might will transform them into all they are meant to be. Help me to reach out with a love that declares that they are *"accepted in the beloved"* (Ephesians 1:6).

In Jesus' name,

The Lord's Answer/s to Me

PART III

TEARING DOWN SPECIFIC STRONGHOLDS

Day 23

"I'm About As Good As Anyone Else"

But we are all as an unclean thing, and all our righteousnesses are as filthy rags; and we all do fade as a leaf; and our iniquities, like the wind, have taken us away.   Isaiah 64:6

Many people are convinced that they simply don't need Jesus. Their attitude may include thoughts like, "I live a good enough life," "I'm about as good as anyone else," or "I haven't really done anything all that bad." Pride and self-righteousness are the roots to this type of thinking. Before speaking with people who have this attitude, it helps to spend some time in humble prayer, pulling down these strongholds on their behalf—if you're to have any hope of influencing them for Christ.

Ask the Lord to shine His light upon their hearts, exposing areas of sin. Ask the Holy Spirit to bring conviction and then grant a repentant heart. Ask that the blinders which prevent them from seeing their need be lifted and that the eyes of their understanding be opened. Your patience, prayer and perseverance, combined with the power of Jesus Christ, will result in tearing down these strongholds of self-righteousness and bringing these people to the feet of the Savior.

> ## SCRIPTURE KEYS TO DECLARE
>
> **James 2:10:**
> *For whosoever shall keep the whole law, and yet offend in one point, he is guilty of all.*
>
> **Isaiah 53:6:**
> *All we like sheep have gone astray; we have turned every one to his own way; and the L*ORD *hath laid on him the iniquity of us all.*
>
> **Matthew 5:20:**
> *Except your righteousness shall exceed the righteousness of the scribes and Pharisees, ye shall in no case enter into the kingdom of heaven.*

Harvesting Souls

POINTS TO PONDER

Tearing Down Self-Righteousness

1. Read 2 Corinthians 10:4-5: *"For the weapons of our warfare are not carnal, but mighty through God to the pulling down of strong holds; casting down imaginations, and every high thing that exalteth itself against the knowledge of God, and bringing into captivity every thought to the obedience of Christ."* List some of the statements of self-righteousness and pride you've heard while witnessing to others:

   _____
   _____
   _____
   _____

2. Have you ever struggled with self-righteousness and pride yourself? How did Jesus help you overcome them?

   _____
   _____
   _____
   _____

3. Why do you think fervent, humble prayer may help break self-righteousness and pride in the people to whom you witness?

   _____
   _____
   _____
   _____

Awakening to the Heartbeat of God

My Prayer from the Heart

Heavenly Father,

Give me a heart that will not argue and strive with people who are simply struggling with You. Grant me a humble heart, one that is willing to pray for hardened hearts to soften and prideful hearts to become humble. As others prayed for *me*, help me now to be willing to intercede for others.

In Jesus' name,

The Lord's Answer/s to Me

_____

_____

_____

_____

Day 24

"I Do Good Things for the Community"

But these are written, that ye might believe that Jesus is the Christ, the Son of God; and that believing ye might have life through his name. John 20:31

Sometimes the people we witness to may have religious strongholds, preventing a true salvation experience with Jesus Christ. Some actually believe that living a good life is enough. They feel saved, yet they've never asked Jesus to be their Lord and Savior. A helpful strategy to breaking down these religious strongholds is to explain that our salvation is not based on any good works we might do. It is based only on what Jesus has already done for us. Our salvation is not something we earn through doing; it comes about through believing and receiving what Jesus has done because He loves us.

One of the evidences that someone has truly received Christ is that they will confess Him as Lord and Savior. Romans 10:9-10 declares: *"That if thou shalt confess with thy mouth the Lord Jesus, and shalt believe in thine heart that God hath raised him from the dead, thou shalt be saved. For with the heart man believeth unto righteousness; and with the mouth confession is made unto salvation."* Someone who is busy with good works needs to stop and receive the good work that Jesus accomplished for them on the cross—salvation.

Even with those who may already "feel" saved, share the Scriptures and a prayer for salvation so they can truly become born again into the Kingdom of God.

SCRIPTURE KEYS TO DECLARE

John 3:3:
Verily, verily, I say unto thee, except a man be born again, he cannot see the kingdom of God.

John 5:24:
Verily, verily I say unto you, he that heareth my word, and believeth on him that sent me, hath everlasting life, and shall not come into condemnation; but is passed from death unto life.

John 1:12:
But as many as received him, to them gave he power to become the sons of God, even to them that believe on his name.

Harvesting Souls

POINTS TO PONDER

Doing vs. Being

1. List as many good works as you can think of:

_____
_____
_____
_____

2. How would you explain to someone that good works are not what gains us entrance into Heaven?

_____
_____
_____
_____

3. Although good deeds are important, a personal relationship with Jesus Christ shifts our focus to being Christlike in our behavior. The Bible teaches us to be kind, to love and to be forgiving. *Doing* is important, but *being* is all about character. List other Christlike characteristics encouraged in the Bible:

_____
_____
_____
_____

Awakening to the Heartbeat of God

My Prayer from the Heart

Heavenly Father,

Help me to be a witness to those who are trying to work their way to Heaven. Help me to tell them about Your love, Your forgiveness and the complete work of salvation accomplished at Calvary. Help me to teach others the balance that You bring between doing and being. Most of all, help me to encourage others to be united to You, abiding in the Vine. You are that vine, and we will truly produce fruitful lives only through a relationship with You. Lead me to help those who *feel* saved to truly *be* saved by giving their hearts to You.

In Jesus' name,

The Lord's Answer/s to Me

_____

_____

_____

_____

Day 25

"I Already Belong to a Church"

Neither is there salvation in any other: for there is none other name under heaven given among men, whereby we must be saved. Acts 4:12

Sometimes, when we try to share with people about Jesus, they quickly tell us they already go to church, and some name their denomination: "I'm a Catholic" or "I'm Lutheran," or whatever their church may be. The stronghold is the belief that all they need is a church. A more accurate belief is that attending church becomes more meaningful when we have a personal relationship with Jesus Christ.

Think of an electric lamp. The lamp represents the church, and the light bulb in the lamp represents Jesus. Just as a light bulb provides the lamp with light, Jesus is our Source of light—for the Church and for the world. And, when we individually ask Him to become our Lord and Savior, He becomes our personal light.

Asking Jesus into our hearts is like plugging the electrical cord of a lamp into the power source. Therefore people who want to be a source of light and power in their church can be encouraged to turn to Him. He will give them power, through the Holy Spirit.

Attending church is always a good thing to do, however our heavenly Father wants us to reflect Him to the world, not a church. Therefore He gave us Jesus to be our Source of light and power. When we belong to Jesus, we will shine His light in the church and in the world around us.

SCRIPTURE KEYS TO DECLARE

1 John 1:5 and 7:
This then is the message which we have heard of him, and declare unto you, that God is light, and in him is no darkness at all.
But if we walk in the light, as he is in the light, we have fellowship one with another, and the blood of Jesus Christ his Son cleanseth us from all sin.

John 3:5-7:
Jesus answered, Verily, Verily, I say unto thee, except a man be born of water and of the Spirit, he cannot enter into the kingdom of God. That which is born of the flesh is flesh; and that which is born of the Spirit is spirit. Marvel not that I said unto thee, ye must be born again.

John 8:12:
Then spake Jesus again unto them, saying, I am the light of the world: he that followeth me shall not walk in darkness, but shall have the light of life.

Harvesting Souls

POINTS TO PONDER

Light for the Lamp

1. Read Matthew 25:1-12. The wise virgins kept their lamps full of oil by abiding in Christ. List some ways that we maintain our relationship with Him:
   _____
   _____
   _____
   _____

2. How can a close relationship with Jesus actually improve our relationship with the church we attend?
   _____
   _____
   _____
   _____

3. Explain to someone the analogy of the lamp, light bulb and electric outlet. What was their response?
   _____
   _____
   _____
   _____

My Prayer from the Heart

Heavenly Father,

Help me to teach others that individuals, as well as the church as a whole, need You to be their Source of power and light. Just as You were sent to this world to be a light for all to see, help me to teach others to ask You to be the light within their own hearts. Help me to teach others Your Word which declares: *"Let your light so shine before men, that they may see your good works, and glorify your Father which is in heaven"* (Matthew 5:16).

In Jesus' name,

The Lord's Answer/s to Me

_____

_____

_____

_____

Day 26

"It All Sounds So Foolish"

The natural man receiveth not the things of the Spirit of God: for they are foolishness unto him: neither can he know them, because they are spiritually discerned.
1 Corinthians 2:14

Some people think of the Bible and witnessing for Jesus as foolishness. We need to remember what Paul taught the Corinthians. The truth of God's Word also states: *"The fool hath said in his heart, there is no God. They are corrupt, they have done abominable works, there is none that doeth good"* (Psalm 14:1).

Our natural, human wisdom would tell us not to reach out to those who consider our faith to be foolishness, yet God's amazing grace tells us: *"It pleased God by the foolishness of preaching to save them that believe. ... The foolishness of God is wiser than men; and the weakness of God is stronger than men"* (1 Corinthians 1:21 and 25). With God's grace, let your witness be like an arrow that will **AIM** for the heart of the skeptic.

A = Accept   **I** = Invite   **M** = Motivate

Accept the person's viewpoint. Then remind him that no matter what he thinks, God's love is still there for him.

Awakening to the Heartbeat of God

Invite the person to ask God to change his heart. Tell him that as foolish as it may seem, God will open his eyes and his heart to understand His love and that there's a standing invitation for him to come to the Lord. Finally, **motivate** the person with a sincere testimony of how the love of Jesus has been real in your life.

SCRIPTURE KEYS TO DECLARE

1 Corinthians 1:18:
For the preaching of the cross is to them that perish foolishness; but unto us which are saved it is the power of God.

2 Corinthians 4:3-4:
But if our gospel be hid, it is hid to them that are lost; in whom the god of this world hath blinded the minds of them which believe not, lest the light of the glorious gospel of Christ, who is the image of God, should shine unto them.

Psalm 119:18:
Open thou mine eyes, that I may behold wondrous things out of thy law.

Hebrews 3:15:
Today if ye will hear his voice, harden not your hearts.

Harvesting Souls

POINTS TO PONDER:

It Takes Grace to Combat Foolishness

1. Write down some examples of times when God's grace was strong enough to drive foolishness out of your life.

_____
_____
_____
_____

2. Sometimes people choose not to reach out to God when they need Him most. Think of the following situations and write down how the Holy Spirit would lead you to be a witness to someone who has: lost a loved one, suffered divorce, is being abused, has an addiction (drugs, alcohol, cigarettes, etc.), is suffering from financial problems, is struggling with the guilt of having an abortion, is being rejected or has become rebellious. List other examples that come to you:

_____
_____
_____
_____

3. How should you **AIM** for the heart of someone who thinks your faith is foolish?
   Accept _____
   Invite _____
   Motivate _____

My Prayer from the Heart

Heavenly Father,

Many people thought that when You went to the cross, it was foolishness. Still, You loved unconditionally and declared, *"Father, forgive them; for they know not what they do"* (Luke 23:34). Grant me the grace to **accept** people with Your unconditional love, **invite** them to allow You to change their hearts, and **motivate** them with sincere testimonies. Your Word promises that we overcome Satan by the blood of the lamb and the word of our testimonies (Revelation 12:11). Help me to stir faith in people's hearts and then trust the power of Your Holy Spirit to open their hearts to receive.

In Jesus' name,

The Lord's Answer/s to Me

Day 27

"It Didn't Work for Me"

Of a truth I perceive that God is no respecter of persons: but in every nation he that feareth him, and worketh righteousness, is accepted with him. Acts 10:34-35

Occasionally I hear someone say, "I asked Jesus to come into my heart, but it didn't work for me." The question to use to shatter this stronghold is this: How much of your heart did you allow Jesus to occupy? It's an important question.

A few years ago, a friend of mine offered to bless me by coming over and cleaning my house. I accepted her offer with a grateful heart and allowed her to come to my house and clean. The result was a clean and orderly home. Now, what if I had allowed this friend to come into my home, yet I had only given her permission to clean the front hallway? If I expected to then have a clean, orderly home, I would have been disappointed. In the same way, when we ask Jesus to come into our hearts, He will clean and organize only those areas that we grant Him permission to. If we fail to yield our hearts to His Lordship, we cannot expect His righteousness, peace and joy to take up residence fully in our hearts.

When any person says, "I tried Jesus, and it didn't work for me," encourage them to yield to Him more fully. Remind them that Jesus will never give up on us, however that He also asks that we never give up on Him. He will respond to our faith and increase in our lives in the same measure that we decrease in our tendency to withhold our hearts from Him. To the extent that we give Him access into our hearts, the joy of the Lord will be our strength (see Nehemiah 8:10). When we yield the situations of our lives to Him, we also discover that His *"yoke is easy,"* and His *"burden is light"* (Matthew 11:30).

SCRIPTURE KEYS TO DECLARE

Jeremiah 29:13:
And ye shall seek me, and find me, when ye shall search for me with all your heart

Hebrews 11:6:
But without faith it is impossible to please him; for he that cometh to God must believe that he is, and that he is a rewarder of them that diligently seek him.

Matthew 5:8:
Blessed are the pure in heart: for they shall see God.

Mark 12:30-31:
And thou shalt love the Lord thy God with all thy heart, and with all thy soul, and with all thy mind, and with all thy strength: this is the first commandment. And the second is like, namely this, Thou shalt love thy neighbour as thyself. There is none other commandment greater than these.

Harvesting Souls

POINTS TO PONDER

With the Whole Heart

1. Draw a picture of a heart. Now shade in the amount of your heart that you've already given to Jesus. What areas of your life do you still need to yield to Him?
   _____
   _____
   _____

2. Now, draw two hearts. Explain to someone that when we ask Jesus into our heart, He will occupy the portions of our heart that we yield to Him. Ask that person if he or she has allowed Jesus to come into their heart. Openly share with them how Jesus has influenced your life since you allowed Him to occupy your heart. Draw several crosses in the heart and explain that to the extent that we allow Jesus to live in our hearts, to that same extent we will be able to discover His righteousness, peace and joy. Did you do it? Yes ___ No ___

3. What would you say to someone who has given up on Jesus? If you're not sure, pray and ask the Holy Spirit to give you wisdom, and then list your answers:
   _____
   _____
   _____
   _____

My Prayer from the Heart

Heavenly Father,

Help me to encourage others to love You with their whole heart, soul and mind and to look to You, for You are the Author and Finisher of their faith. As they look to You, may You order their steps and grant them peace.

In Jesus' name,

The Lord's Answer/s to Me

_____

_____

_____

_____

Day 28

"How Do I Know That What the Bible Says Is True?"

Thy word is truth.   John 17:17

As a child, I came to believe that God's Word was true, and yet I was well into my adult years before I started to actually exercise my faith. The reason is that it was only then that I allowed God to change me through His Word.

We're all born with faith to believe in God, and that includes believing in the entire Word of God as found in the Bible. And we're given the faith we need to receive Jesus as our Lord and Savior. The problem is that we're also given the gift of free will. We can exercise our God-given faith and receive Jesus as Lord and Savior, or we can reject Him. It's up to us.

We can also freely choose to receive God's Word and apply it to our lives, or we can choose to reject it and live out the consequences of our own faulty choices. Sometimes we simply need to stir into people their God-given faith to receive His Son Jesus and His precious Word.

Tell them that one small seed of faith is all that's needed to remove mountains of doubt and that simply calling on the name of Jesus can quickly remove the mountains of disappointment, resentment, fear, rebellion and discouragement built up in them through the circumstances of

Awakening to the Heartbeat of God

life. Ask them the question: "Would you like to exercise your faith and give God the chance to confirm His Word to you personally?" Assure them that He will do *"exceeding abundantly above all that we can ask or think"* (Ephesians 3:20). Simply say, "Got faith? Try Jesus!"

SCRIPTURE KEYS TO DECLARE

John 20:31:
But these are written, that ye might believe that Jesus is the Christ, the Son of God; and that believing ye might have life through his name.

Ephesians 3:14-19:
For this cause I bow my knees unto the Father of our Lord Jesus Christ, of whom the whole family in heaven and earth is named, that he would grant you, according to the riches of his glory, to be strengthened with might by his Spirit in the inner man; that Christ may dwell in your hearts by faith; that ye, being rooted and grounded in love, may be able to comprehend with all saints what is the breadth, and length, and depth, and height; and to know the love of Christ, which passeth knowledge, that ye might be filled with all the fulness of God.

Matthew 17:20:
If ye have faith as a grain of mustard seed, ye shall say unto this mountain, remove hence to yonder place; and it shall remove; and nothing shall be impossible unto you.

Harvesting Souls

POINTS TO PONDER

Exercise Your Faith Muscle

1. Have you ever had times when you had difficulty believing God's Word? What caused you to respond in faith?

   _____
   _____
   _____
   _____

2. Write down some testimonies of times when God responded to your seeds of faith, exceeding abundantly more than you could have ever asked for:

   _____
   _____
   _____
   _____

3. List some of life's circumstances that would cause a person to want to doubt God's Word. How would you minister encouragement and faith to people walking through those very situations?

   _____
   _____
   _____
   _____

My Prayer from the Heart

Heavenly Father,

Your Word states: *"Now abideth faith, hope, charity [love in action], these three; but the greatest of these is charity"* (1 Corinthians 13:13). Help me to be a vessel of Your light, stirring faith and hope in others. Help me to stir faith, encouraging people to receive You as Lord and Savior. Help me to stir hope, encouraging others to apply Your Word to their lives. Help me to walk in charity, demonstrating love in action to a world that needs kindness and goodness to draw them to You.

In Jesus' name,

The Lord's Answer/s to Me

_____

_____

_____

_____

Day 29

"Help! I Have Unforgiveness!"

For if ye forgive men their trespasses, your heavenly Father will also forgive you: but if ye forgive not men their trespasses, neither will your Father forgive your trespasses. Matthew 6:14-15

Often people we witness to sincerely want to receive Jesus as Lord and Savior, but they have a problem with unforgiveness. Some are angry with God. A tragic death, a rebellious child or sudden unemployment are just a few of the many life challenges that may cause someone to blame God. But God is never to blame for our difficulties.

Many cannot receive the forgiveness of Christ because they harbor bitterness toward some other person who has hurt them in some way. Share with them the scriptures on this subject. Unforgiveness will prevent us from having God's blessings upon our lives. It helps to assure people that when we forgive others of the sins they have committed toward us, our hearts are then set free to receive the forgiveness that God extends to us.

Possibly the most challenging stronghold of unforgiveness to tear down is the unforgiveness of oneself. It helps to remind people that if God can forgive us of our sins, we are actually placing ourselves above Him if we're then not willing to forgive ourselves.

Whatever type of unforgiveness people may struggle with, encourage them, using God's promises, to forgive with childlike faith—whether or not they have feelings of forgiveness. In response to their childlike faith, they will see the stronghold of unforgiveness shattered, and the outstretched arms of Jesus will become real in their lives.

Scripture Keys to Declare

Luke 6:36-37:
Be ye therefore merciful, as your Father also is merciful. Judge not, and ye shall not be judged: condemn not, and ye shall not be condemned: forgive, and ye shall be forgiven.

Matthew 6:12:
And forgive us our debts, as we forgive our debtors.

Psalm 86:5:
For thou, Lord, art good, and ready to forgive; and plenteous in mercy unto all them that call upon thee.

POINTS TO PONDER

Let's Talk About Forgiveness

1. List examples of unforgiveness in your life—toward God, toward others and toward yourself:
   _____
   _____
   _____
   _____

2. How did the love of Jesus help you to extend forgiveness in these situations?
   _____
   _____
   _____
   _____

3. Have you ever ministered to someone who was struggling with unforgiveness? Ask the Holy Spirit to bring ideas to you on how to help people let go of their unforgiveness. List some of His answers here:
   _____
   _____
   _____
   _____

My Prayer from the Heart

Heavenly Father,

I know that unforgiveness can be a stumbling block to receiving Your love and forgiveness. Help me to be a source of encouragement to others to release unforgiveness from their hearts. Help me to remind them of Your promises. Equip me to teach others to extend forgiveness to themselves and others and to receive forgiveness from You.

In Jesus' name,

The Lord's Answer/s to Me

_____

_____

_____

_____

Day 30

"If God Is So Good, Why Do So Many Bad Things Happen in the World?"

These things I have spoken unto you, that in me ye might have peace. In the world ye shall have tribulation: but be of good cheer; I have overcome the world.

John 16:33

It's surprising how many people struggle with all the evil that exists in our world. Their question is something like this: "If God is so loving, why does He allow so much evil?" The answer is that God created mankind with the ability to choose good or evil. To the extent that people choose to follow God's ways and His Word, they contribute to good in the world. To the extent that men rebel against His Word, they contribute to the evils all around us. There's an answer for the evil of this world, and that answer can be found in a personal relationship with Jesus Christ.

Those who abide in Christ contribute righteousness, peace and joy to the world around them. Abiding in Him also gives them the peace they need to live in such a world, a world that does, in fact, contain much evil. Jesus said it would be so.

This reminds me of the very powerful phrase: "No

Jesus? No peace! Know Jesus? Know peace!" Encourage others to know Jesus personally, and they will come to know His eternal peace, whatever happens in the world around them.

> ### SCRIPTURE KEYS TO DECLARE
>
> **Numbers 6:24-26:**
> *The Lord bless thee, and keep thee: the Lord make his face shine upon thee, and be gracious unto thee: the Lord lift up his countenance upon thee, and give thee peace.*
>
> **Psalm 4:8:**
> *I will both lay me down in peace, and sleep: for thou, Lord, only makest me dwell in safety.*
>
> **Philippians 4:6-7:**
> *Be careful for nothing; but in every thing by prayer and supplication with thanksgiving let your requests be made known unto God. And the peace of God, which passeth all understanding, shall keep your hearts and minds through Christ Jesus.*

Harvesting Souls

POINTS TO PONDER

Living in Peace in Our Stress-Filled World

1. List some typical news items you might see on TV news or in your local newspaper:

   _____
   _____
   _____
   _____

2. Do you think that a person could better cope with the stresses of this life with Jesus or without Him? Explain your answer:

   _____
   _____
   _____
   _____

3. Have you ever felt the peace of God during challenging times in your life? How would you witness to others about this peace?

   _____
   _____
   _____
   _____

Awakening to the Heartbeat of God

My Prayer from the Heart

Heavenly Father,

You are the Prince of Peace, so You can give us peace—even in the midst of life's storms. Help me to be a source of peace to the world around me and help me to witness to others that no matter what occurs in this world, You are our Refuge, our Rock and our Source of peace.

In Jesus' name,

The Lord's Answer/s to Me

_____

_____

_____

_____

Part IV

Putting on Daddy's Shoes

Day 31

Shoes of Faith

For we walk by faith, not by sight. 2 Corinthians 5:7

Children love to put on their father's shoes. It gives them a sense of power and authority. As Christians, we can put on our heavenly Father's shoes—with all that it signifies. When we submit our lives to God through Jesus Christ, our feelings of human inadequacy are replaced with an understanding that we are walking in our Father's authority, and we are being guided by His Holy Spirit.

When we're reaching out to the world with the Good News of Jesus, one pair of shoes we need to walk in would be the shoes of faith. What are some scriptural principles we could apply in order to activate the shoes of faith? Let's think a moment of the three-way-reach-out-in-faith plan:

#1 Reach up with our hands to our heavenly Father. Whether we're in prayer, praise or worship, lifting our hands to God reminds us to reach toward Him and His promises. Psalm 63:4 states: *"Thus will I bless thee while I live: I will lift up my hands in thy name."* When we lift our hands to God, He pours into us faith and the ability to walk in His power and authority.

#2 Reach out with words of faith. Such words can be generated through speaking the Word of God, and they can also occur when we pray in agreement with the Holy Spirit. We should all follow the scriptural principle: *"pray without ceasing"* (1 Thessalonians 5:17).

Awakening to the Heartbeat of God

#3 Reach out with your spirit. Faith is built up in our inner man (the spirit man) when we reach out to God by praying in the Spirit.

As you exercise the three-way-reach-out-in-faith plan, your heavenly Father empowers you to walk in His shoes of faith. And with those shoes of faith in place, expect to see breakthroughs—miracles and salvations in the harvest fields of your life.

SCRIPTURE KEYS TO DECLARE

Matthew 18:19-20:
If two of you shall agree on earth as touching any thing that they shall ask, it shall be done for them of my Father which is in heaven. For where two or three are gathered together in my name, there am I in the midst of them.

Matthew 4:4:
But He [Jesus] answered and said, It is written, Man shall not live by bread alone, but by every word that proceedeth out of the mouth of God.

1 Thessalonians 5:17:
Pray without ceasing.

Jude 20:
But ye, beloved, building up yourselves on your most holy faith, praying in the Holy Ghost.

Harvesting Souls

POINTS TO PONDER

The Three-way-Reach-Out-in-Faith Plan

1. Lift up those hands! Spend some time worshiping the Lord, with hands outstretched to Him. Praise Him for the miracles of salvation you have witnessed in your life. Then, praise Him, declaring that He is the God of salvation for your current harvest fields.
Did you do it? Yes ___ No ___

2. Reach out with words of faith. Here are a couple of faith-filled scriptures you can use: *"All flesh shall see the salvation of God"* (Luke 3:6). *"Wherefore he is able also to save them to the uttermost that come unto God by him, seeing he ever liveth to make intercession for them"* (Hebrews 7:25). List other scriptures that activate your shoes of faith to be a witness for Christ:

_____
_____
_____
_____

3. Dedicate some time each day to pray in the Spirit for the people whom you're believing to be saved. How does praying in the Spirit activate your shoes of faith?

_____
_____
_____
_____

Awakening to the Heartbeat of God

My Prayer from the Heart

Heavenly Father,

I want to be a witness to the world for Your Son, Jesus Christ. Activate my shoes of faith to walk boldly into the harvest fields You would send me to. Help me to be a willing witness declaring, *"Here am I; send me!"* Help me reach up to You with arms of faith, as well as speak and pray words of faith to others. Please strengthen my faith, as I pray in the power of Your Holy Spirit.

In Jesus' name,

The Lord's Answer/s to Me

_____

_____

_____

_____

Day 32

Shoes of Christlike Character

This I say then, Walk in the Spirit, and ye shall not fulfil the lust of the flesh.   Galatians 5:16

Have you heard the phrase, "Let your walk speak louder than your talk?" The character we demonstrate to the people who surround us will influence them far more than any words we might say.

How can we activate shoes of Christlike character? Remember first that putting on a display of Christlike character will require a desire to obey God's will. As we submit our hearts to follow godly principals, our actions will activate Christlike character.

Christlike character will be seen when we walk in love. Paul reminded us: *"Charity [love] never faileth"* (1 Corinthians 13:8). When we humble ourselves, our heavenly Father also displays in us those shoes of Christlike character. James wrote to the Church: *"Humble yourselves in the sight of the Lord, and he shall lift you up"* (James 4:10).

The easiest way to remember how to activate shoes of Christlike character would be to simply walk in the Spirit and do the opposite of what Satan tries to provoke us to do. If someone walks in unkind shoes, you choose to walk in forgiveness. For those who would curse you or persecute

Awakening to the Heartbeat of God

you, choose to bless them instead. Always think of Jesus' words: *"Love your enemies, bless them that curse you, do good to them that hate you, and pray for them which despitefully use you, and persecute you"* (Matthew 4:44).

God's children, walking in shoes of Christlike character, need to be seen even more than they need to be heard. Submit to God's way, and you will become a lighthouse for all to see.

Scripture Keys to Declare

1 John 4:11-12:
Beloved, if God so loved us, we ought also to love one another. If we love one another, God dwelleth in us, and his love is perfected in us.

Mark 11:25-26:
And when ye stand praying, forgive, if ye have aught against any that your Father also which is in heaven may forgive you your trespasses. But if ye do not forgive, neither will your Father which is in heaven forgive your trespasses.

1 Thessalonians 5:15:
See that none render evil for evil unto any man; but ever follow that which is good, both among yourselves, and to all men.

Harvesting Souls

POINTS TO PONDER

Stepping into Shoes of Christlike Character

1. Rate yourself with the following list of Christlike behaviors. How many of these behaviors do you walk in on a regular basis? Respect for authority ___, forgiveness ___, generosity ___, words of kindness ___, love for the unlovable ___ and servanthood ___.
   List other behaviors:

   _____
   _____
   _____

2. How quickly do you forgive someone who has wronged you? How does forgiveness demonstrate Christlike character?

   _____
   _____
   _____
   _____

3. What are some significant ways to bless those who would curse you?

   _____
   _____
   _____
   _____

My Prayer from the Heart

Heavenly Father,

I know that I need to step into shoes of Christlike character to make a difference in the world around me. Help me to put Christlike love into action. Help me to fully submit to Your ways, which are higher and wiser than my ways. Help me to be a blessing to others, as I humble myself before You. As I am able to activate shoes of Christlike character, then my walk will be a louder witness than my talk.

In Jesus' name,

The Lord's Answer/s to Me

_____

_____

_____

_____

Day 33

The Shoes of a Warrior

Upon this rock I will build my church; and the gates of hell shall not prevail against it. And I will give unto thee the keys of the kingdom of heaven, and whatsoever thou shalt bind on earth shall be bound in heaven: and whatsoever thou shalt loose on earth shall be loosed in heaven.

Matthew 16:18-19

Shoes are an important source of protection for our bodies. If we had to go without them, many things we encounter daily along the way would hurt us. When we enter our harvest fields, we can activate the protective shoes of a warrior by applying scriptural principles that shield us from the evil plans of Satan.

Activate your warrior shoes with your hands, your mouth and your prayers: Clap your hands before the Lord, declaring that the enemy is defeated. Psalm 47:1 states: *"O clap your hands, all ye people; shout unto God with the voice of triumph."* With your mouth, declare that the blood of Jesus enters your harvest fields, defeating the enemy and bringing forth God's plan for salvation. Colossians 1:20 states: *"And, having made peace through the blood of his cross, by him to reconcile all things unto himself."* In your prayers, apply the name of Jesus and the principles of binding and loosing. Just as we can clean out a path of anything that might hurt us, we can spiritually clean out a path into our harvest fields, by binding up the enemy and then loosing, or calling forth, God's plans and purposes. When we apply this principle in the mighty name of Jesus, that name and the power of it will *"spoil [defeat] principalities and powers, making a show of them openly, triumphing over them"* (Colossians 2:15).

SCRIPTURE KEYS TO DECLARE

Ephesians 6:10-17:
Finally, my brethren, be strong in the Lord, and in the power of his might. Put on the whole armour of God, that ye may be able to stand against the wiles of the devil. ... Stand therefore, having your loins girt about with truth, and having on the breastplate of righteousness; and your feet shod with the preparation of the gospel of peace; above all, taking the shield of faith, wherewith ye shall be able to quench all the fiery darts of the wicked. And take the helmet of salvation, and the sword of the Spirit, which is the word of God.

Mark 16:17-18:
And these signs shall follow them that believe; In my name shall they cast out devils; they shall speak with new tongues; they shall take up serpents; and if they drink any deadly thing, it shall not hurt them; they shall lay hands on the sick, and they shall recover.

Romans 8:37:
Nay, in all these things we are more than conquerors through him that loved us.

Harvesting Souls

POINTS TO PONDER

Step with the Shoes of a Warrior for Winning Souls

1. Read Ephesians 6:10-17. Do you always put on the armor of God? How can it make a difference in your day?

___
___
___

2. Here are some harmful spirits that can be cleaned out of our harvest fields through focused prayer: pride, religious attitudes, independence, shame, unforgiveness, rebellion and self-righteousness.
List others:

___
___
___

3. Describe times when you've prayed over situations before witnessing for Jesus. How does prayer help prepare the way for people to receive your witness for Him?

___
___
___
___

My Prayer from the Heart

Heavenly Father,

We are called to be soldiers for the army of God. Help me to be willing to wear the shoes of a warrior. Give me the discipline to put on the armor of God and the wisdom to use the principles of binding and loosing. Help me understand that there's power in Your name, and Your reconciling love is found in Your precious blood. As I wear the shoes of a warrior, help me to have victory in winning souls for Your Kingdom.

In Jesus' name,

The Lord's Answer/s to Me

_____

_____

_____

_____

Day 34

Shoes of Victory

And when he [Jehoshaphat] had consulted with the people, he appointed singers unto the LORD, and that should praise the beauty of holiness, as they went out before the army, and to say, Praise the LORD; for his mercy endureth for ever. 2 Chronicles 20:21

When the Lord of the Harvest sends us into the harvest fields, we need to be wearing His shoes of victory. We can then expect breakthroughs anywhere we go, and we can also expect to shatter strongholds of darkness with the light of Jesus Christ.

Before entering your harvest fields, activate the shoes of victory through thanksgiving and praise to the Lord. Singing before Him, shouting His praises and dancing before Him all bring defeat to the enemy and victory for God's Kingdom. The time you spend with the Lord in thanksgiving, praise, song, dance and shouts of victory will be multiplied back to you, as the Holy Spirit goes before you to prepare the hearts of the people you are intending to reach.

Apply God's tools, shout the victory and see the walls of resistance come tumbling down before you. See with the Father's eyes, light shattering darkness, and souls coming forth into His Kingdom. Do you have on your shoes of victory? Then, let's march!

Scripture Keys to Declare

Joshua 6:20:
So the people shouted when the priests blew with the trumpets: and it came to pass, when the people heard the sound of the trumpet, and the people shouted with a great shout, that the wall fell down flat, so that the people went up into the city, every man straight before him, and they took the city.

Psalm 100:4:
Enter his gates with thanksgiving, and into his courts with praise: be thankful unto him, and bless his name.

Psalm 149:5-6:
Let the saints be joyful in glory: let them sing aloud upon their beds. Let the high praises of God be in their mouth, and a two-edged sword in their hand.

Exodus 15:20-21:
And Miriam the prophetess, the sister of Aaron, took a timbrel in her hand, and all the women went out after her with timbrels and with dances. And Miriam answered them, Sing ye to the Lord, for he hath triumphed gloriously; the horse and his rider hath he thrown into the sea.

Harvesting Souls

POINTS TO PONDER

Preparing for Victory

1. List times when you have applied these scriptural principles prior to entering into your harvest fields: thanksgiving, praise, shouts of victory, dance and song. List others that you've used:

_____
_____
_____
_____

2. Describe times when you've seen the Spirit of our Lord shatter walls of resistance ... :

In your own life:_____

In other people:_____

In your workplace:_____

In your community:_____

3. List some worldly habits to avoid because they would tend to encourage defeat, rather than victory:

_____
_____
_____
_____

My Prayer from the Heart

Heavenly Father,

Your Word tells us to see that the harvest fields are *"white unto harvest,"* meaning that the people who need our witness are ready and willing to come into Your Kingdom. I thank You and praise You for preparing hearts in my harvest field. Stir my faith to know that as I sing and dance before You and shout Your victory, I will indeed see walls of resistance coming down and souls being won for Your Kingdom.

In Jesus' name,

The Lord's Answer/s to Me

Part V

Nurturing New Babies

Day 35

The Miracle of New Birth

Therefore if any man be in Christ, he is a new creature.
2 Corinthians 5:17

There is so much excitement when a mother is preparing for her baby to be born. She spends time in prayer, eats and rests well and deals with any challenges as they arise. The process is similar when we cooperate with our heavenly Father, as the Holy Spirit births new spiritual babies into the Kingdom of God.

As you have been reading these devotions, following through with the questions and prayers, and then attempting to be a better witness in your harvest fields, have you been blessed to see someone born again into a relationship with Jesus Christ? Do you see hearts softening to the Good News? All your efforts—to pray, feed on God's Word and then reach out to a needy world—will eventually make a difference. Rest in God's promises, and seek His wisdom for times of challenge. Our labors and the demonstration of Christlike character hold much promise for the miracle of new births in the Kingdom.

What happens when our faith-filled efforts result in seeing someone born again? As the song would say, at that point, "We have only just begun!" Just as a new baby needs nourishment, love and prayer, so it is for those born into the Kingdom of God. We would never abandon a newborn baby, and we must not spiritually abandon a newborn child of God. Ask the Father not only for faith to see new births into the Kingdom of God, but also for the love, understanding and discipline to be vessels who will show these new spiritual babes how to live in Him.

SCRIPTURE KEYS TO DECLARE

2 Peter 3:9:
The Lord is not slack concerning his promise, as some men count slackness; but is longsuffering to us-ward, not willing that any should perish, but that all should come to repentance.

Ephesians 1:6:
To the praise of the glory of his grace, wherein he hath made us accepted in the beloved.

1 John 3:16-18:
Hereby perceive we the love of God, because he laid down his life for us: and we ought to lay down our lives for the brethren. But whoso hath this world's good, and seeth his brother have need, and shutteth up his bowels of compassion from him, how dwelleth the love of God in him? My little children, let us not love in word, neither in tongue; but in deed and in truth.

Harvesting Souls

POINTS TO PONDER

Taking Care of a Baby

1. Think of a newborn baby, and then think of a new baby in Christ. Look at what a new infant needs, and then list what a new infant in Christ needs.

A Newborn Infant	A New Infant in Christ
Nourishment	_____
Comfort	_____
Constant care	_____
Parents and family	_____

2. Sometimes a newborn infant will wake us up in the middle of the night or at some other inconvenient time. Describe what you would do if a newly born-again believer were to call you in the middle of the night or at some other inconvenient time. And what would Jesus do?

_____
_____
_____

3. What are some ways that you could encourage a new believer to feed on the pure Word of God?

_____
_____
_____

Awakening to the Heartbeat of God

My Prayer from the Heart

Heavenly Father,

Help me to remember that evangelism is only a first step and that we're also called to disciple spiritual newborns. Help me to remember that You spent three years with Your disciples, and that You sacrificed Your life for all mankind. Give me an attitude of parenthood (a mentor's heart) for new believers. Help me to be a vessel that will help them grow in the grace and knowledge of Jesus Christ, our Lord.

In Jesus' name,

The Lord's Answer/s to Me

_____

_____

_____

_____

Day 36

Feed Them

As newborn babes, desire the sincere milk of the word, that ye may grow thereby.   1 Peter 2:2

Have you ever noticed how often a newborn baby feeds? It seems that infants are always hungry. The most natural, God-given method of feeding a new infant is with breast milk. A breast-fed infant receives nourishment, at the same time he receives comfort and security. And the infant will thrive as a result of frequent feedings.

A new babe in Christ can also thrive through frequently feeding on the pure Word of God. They are to *"desire the sincere milk of the Word."* In my case, I was given my first Bible when I was just seven years old, and I thought it was the best book in the entire world. (I still think so!)

How exciting to give a new Christian his or her first Bible, but even more exciting is to teach a new Christian how to feed on the Word of God. Just like children, they need to be taught how to use the Bible, encouraged to attend Bible study and encouraged to attend a church dedicated to preaching the entire Word of God. New believers need those who will give them basic milk—scriptural principles to help them grow and feel secure in their relationship with God.

Awakening to the Heartbeat of God

As you equip new believers to feed on the pure Word of God, you will be blessed to see the process through which they truly become new creations in Christ.

SCRIPTURE KEYS TO DECLARE

1 Timothy 1:14:
And the grace of our Lord was exceeding abundant with faith and love which is in Christ Jesus.

1 Peter 5:2-4:
Feed the flock of God which is among you, taking the oversight thereof, not by constraint, but willingly; not for filthy lucre, but of a ready mind. Neither as being lords over God's heritage, but being ensamples to the flock. And when the chief Shepherd shall appear, ye shall receive a crown of glory that fadeth not away.

John 21:17:
Jesus saith unto him, Feed my sheep.

Harvesting Souls

POINTS TO PONDER

Feeding Those Babies

1. List various ways in which you can help ensure that a new believer feeds on the Word of God.

2. List any memories you have of giving a Bible to someone. Currently, is there someone the Lord would have you give a Bible to?

3. List scriptures that were an encouragement to you when you first received Christ:

4. What would happen if a new believer failed to feed on the Word of God?

My Prayer from the Heart

Heavenly Father,

Remind me of the hunger that I had for Your Word when I first became born again. Help me to be available to new believers, encouraging them with the Bible, explaining scriptures to them and encouraging them to have regular Bible study. Help me to know that just as other people helped feed *me* with Your Word, I can now feed others. Please grant me a mentor's heart, a heart that rejoices to see others growing in Your love and grace.

In Jesus' name,

The Lord's Answer/s to Me

_____

_____

_____

_____

Day 37

Encourage Them to Submit to Water Baptism

Know ye not, that so many of us as were baptized into Jesus Christ were baptized into his death? Therefore we are buried with him by baptism into death: that like as Christ was raised up from the dead by the glory of the Father, even so we also should walk in newness of life.

Romans 6:3-4

Just as a newborn baby is bathed and cleansed, a new spiritual baby is bathed and cleansed by submitting to water baptism. More so, water baptism signifies that the person in question has died (the water is the grave to bury them) and a new person then comes forth. Water baptism is also a witness in which we identify with the death, burial and resurrection of our Lord.

This is an important experience, and God's Word instructs us: *"Go ye therefore, and teach all nations, baptizing them in the name of the Father, and of the Son, and of the Holy Ghost"* (Matthew 28:19).

Water baptism is a public testimony of repentance, demonstrating a heart willing to turn from a worldly life and live for Jesus and His commandments. Acts 2:38 describes the results of water baptism: *"Repent, and be baptized every one of you in the name of Jesus Christ for the remission of sins, and ye shall receive the gift of the Holy Ghost."*

It's so exciting for a parent to wrap a clean and bathed newborn into a warm receiving blanket and hold him or her for the first time. And it's just as exciting to encourage a new believer to submit to water baptism, and then wrap a clean, soft white towel around him. Think of the towel as representing God's pure love and the outstretched arms of the Body of Christ, reaching out to this new babe in Christ. What could be more wonderful?

SCRIPTURE KEYS TO DECLARE

Matthew 3:13-17:
Then cometh Jesus from Galilee to Jordan unto John, to be baptized of him. But John forbad him, saying, I have need to be baptized of thee, and comest thou to me? And Jesus answering said unto him, Suffer it to be so now: for thus it becometh us to fulfil all righteousness. Then he suffered him. And Jesus, when he was baptized, went up straightway out of the water: and, lo, the heavens were opened unto him, and he saw the Spirit of God descending like a dove, and lighting upon him: and lo a voice from heaven, saying, This is my beloved Son, in whom I am well pleased.

Mark 16:16:
He that believeth and is baptized shall be saved.

Harvesting Souls

POINTS TO PONDER

A Bath for New Believers

1. Describe your water baptism. Who taught you about water baptism? And what did you experience after being baptized?

_____
_____
_____
_____

2. How would you encourage a new believer to be baptized in water? List any scriptures that you might feed to a new Christian to help him understand this experience:

_____
_____
_____
_____

3. When I was baptized in water, a few friends in Christ came to witness my baptism, and they then gave me cards of encouragement. Describe other ways you might celebrate a new believer's water baptism.

_____
_____
_____
_____

Awakening to the Heartbeat of God

My Prayer from the Heart

Heavenly Father,

Help me remember to encourage new believers with Your Word concerning water baptism. Remind us all of the powerful testimony water baptism brings forth—testifying to all of Your death, burial and resurrection. Help me to encourage new believers to submit to water baptism, as a testimony of their newness of life in You. You truly wash away the old and raise up the new in us.

In Jesus' name,

The Lord's Answer/s to Me

_____

_____

_____

_____

Day 38

Encourage Them to Receive the Baptism of the Holy Spirit

And, behold, I send the promise of my Father upon you: but tarry ye in the city of Jerusalem, until ye be endued with power from on high. Luke 24:49

When I first became a new believer in Christ, I had many habits and personal issues to conquer. I needed to change, but I needed God's supernatural strength and power to do it. I needed the fire of God to purify me and to stir my heart to be a bold witness for Jesus.

It is important to share with new believers about the fire of God, otherwise known as the baptism of the Holy Spirit. Our heavenly Father promised those who would follow Him: *"But ye shall receive power, after that the Holy Ghost is come upon you: and ye shall be witnesses unto me both in Jerusalem, and in all Judaea, and in Samaria, and unto the uttermost part of the earth"* (Acts 1:8).

Our Lord desires to equip new believers with the full measure they need to grow in Christ, and the baptism of the Holy Spirit provides this full measure. Once we have taught a new believer about both water baptism and the baptism of the Holy Spirit, we will joyfully see this new believer rapidly grow in his or her Christian experience.

Awakening to the Heartbeat of God

Just as a new baby learns to crawl, then walk and finally run, we will also see these steps of growth in the new Christian. Pour on the fire of the Holy Ghost!

SCRIPTURE KEYS TO DECLARE

Luke 3:16:
John [the Baptist] answered, saying unto them all, I indeed baptize you with water; but one mightier than I cometh, the latchet of whose shoes I am not worthy to unloose: he [Jesus] shall baptize you with the Holy Ghost and with fire.

Acts 1:4-5:
And, being assembled together with them [the disciples], commanded them that they should not depart from Jerusalem, but wait for the promise of the Father, which, saith he, ye have heard of me. For John truly baptized with water; but ye shall be baptized with the Holy Ghost not many days hence.

Jude 20-21:
But ye, beloved, building up yourselves on your most holy faith, praying in the Holy Ghost. Keep yourselves in the love of God, looking for the mercy of our Lord Jesus Christ unto eternal life.

Harvesting Souls

POINTS TO PONDER

Fire and Glory

1. Describe what happened when you were baptized in the Holy Spirit. How did it help you grow as a believer in Christ?

   _____
   _____
   _____

2. Talk with someone this week about the baptism of the Holy Spirit. If need be, practice with a friend at church. What was the outcome of your sharing?

   _____
   _____
   _____

3. The baptism of the Holy Spirit provides God's fire to purify our hearts. What are some areas in your life that God has purified?

   _____
   _____
   _____

4. In what ways have you walked in a greater level of God's power, after having received the baptism of the Holy Spirit?

   _____
   _____
   _____

Awakening to the Heartbeat of God

My Prayer from the Heart

Heavenly Father,

Remind me of the fire and glory brought into my life through the baptism of the Holy Spirit. Reveal to me scriptures and ideas on how to witness to new believers about this experience, and give me the opportunity to share with them these truths. Baptize me afresh and new with Your fire and glory, and give me a faithful heart to impart this power to others.

In Jesus' name,

The Lord's Answer/s to Me

Day 39

Teach Them to Pray

And it came to pass, that, as he was praying in a certain place, when he ceased, one of his disciples said unto him, Lord, teach us to pray, as John also taught his disciples.

Luke 11:1

It's always important to teach new believers how to pray. In the beginning, they may tend to look to themselves, to the church or to other Christians, when searching for strength and answers. As they learn to pray, they learn to look to the true Source of wisdom, strength and answers. What, then, are some simple ideas for encouraging new believers to pray? How about showing them the high-five plan?

Hold out to the new Christian your outstretched hand, each finger representing an important truth about prayer: (1.) **Pray simply:** A new believer does not need to be concerned with how much he or she prays, as much as focusing on simple, heartfelt prayer. (2.) **Pray honestly:** Honest conversation with our heavenly Father strengthens our relationship with Him. (3.) **Pray in faith:** Teach new believers to trust in God to hear our prayers and answer according to His will and purposes. (4.) **Pray daily:** Encourage new believers to pray in the morning and before bedtime, but also remind them that any time of day is a great time to pray. (5.) **Pray in the Spirit:** Once a new believer has been baptized in the Holy Spirit, they should then be encouraged to pray in the Spirit.

Once these five points are explained, join your hand with that of the new believer, explaining that you're willing to pray with that person, if and when they need your help. As you encourage new believers with this high-five plan, you will truly see them grow in the grace and knowledge of our Lord Jesus Christ.

SCRIPTURE KEYS TO DECLARE

Psalm 55:17:
Evening, and morning, and at noon, will I pray, and cry aloud: and he shall hear my voice.

Jeremiah 33:3:
Call unto me, and I will answer thee, and show thee great and mighty things, which thou knowest not.

James 5:16:
Confess your faults one to another, and pray one for another, that ye may be healed. The effectual fervent prayer of a righteous man availeth much.

Harvesting Souls

POINTS TO PONDER

Teaching Others to Pray

1. Read Psalm 100:4. List ideas for teaching a new believer to express thanksgiving and praise to God. How do we bless His name?

   _____
   _____
   _____
   _____

2. How much time do you spend in prayer each day? How would you encourage a new believer to pray each morning?

   _____
   _____
   _____
   _____

3. List all the ways that prayer has helped you grow in your relationship with God. What would be your response to a Christian who needs to be encouraged to pray more often?

   _____
   _____
   _____
   _____

Awakening to the Heartbeat of God

My Prayer from the Heart

Heavenly Father,

Help me to remember all the ways that prayer helped me learn to trust in You. Help me to be willing to pray with and encourage new believers. Help me to teach them to pray—daily, simply, honestly, in faith and by Your Spirit. As I encourage them, I trust that I will see them grow in their relationship with You.

In Jesus' name,

The Lord's Answer/s to Me

_____

_____

_____

_____

Day 40

Give Them Room to Grow

But grow in grace, and in the knowledge of our Lord and Saviour Jesus Christ. To him be glory both now and for ever. Amen.   2 Peter 3:18

    Most people seem to think that the best way to help a new believer to grow is to give him or her some "Christian" things to do, but I don't think that's what Jesus would say. His answer would simply be: "Follow Me and abide in Me." If we will counsel new Christians to firmly take Jesus by the hand, He will be their faithful Shepherd.

    Pray and encourage new believers to have eyes that see, ears that hear and a heart that responds to the things that Jesus would have them do. Encourage new believers to read their Bibles, go to church and spend time in prayer. Encourage Christian fellowship. Yet do not let these encouragements become legalistic "shoulds" or "musts." As we encourage new believers to abide in Christ (to develop a heartfelt and sincere relationship with Him) our faithful Shepherd will provide them with a Spirit-led desire to grow spiritually and be connected with the Body of Christ. Your goal for new babies in Christ is to nurture and teach them and yet give them room to grow. Don't do anything that might hold them back.

    As a parent, I sometimes miss my children's infancy

days. Still, as I release them into adulthood, my heart is overwhelmed with joy to realize that their relationship with Christ has to become one of love and trust, not of "shoulds" and "can'ts." Hold those new babies close to your heart and teach and train them. But you must faithfully and fully understand that they do not belong to you. They belong to God. So release them to Him.

Scripture Keys to Declare

Psalm 23:1-3:
The Lord is my shepherd; I shall not want. He maketh me to lie down in green pastures: he leadeth me beside the still waters. He restoreth my soul: he leadeth me in the paths of righteousness for his name's sake.

John 15:4-5:
Abide in me, and I in you. As the branch cannot bear fruit of itself, except it abide in the vine; no more can ye, except ye abide in me. I am the vine, ye are the branches: He that abideth in me, and I in him, the same bringeth forth much fruit: for without me ye can do nothing.

Romans 8:14:
For as many as are led by the Spirit of God, they are the sons of God.

Harvesting Souls

POINTS TO PONDER

Raise Them by the Spirit

1. Think back to when you were a new Christian. How did people encourage you to grow in your relationship with Christ?

   _____
   _____
   _____
   _____

2. List ways that you can encourage other new believers to be connected to the Body of Christ:

   _____
   _____
   _____
   _____

3. List ways to be careful not to impose legalistic attitudes on new Christians. How can you encourage a new Christian to change and grow by loving Jesus, rather than as a response to "shoulds" and "shouldn'ts"?:

   _____
   _____
   _____
   _____

Awakening to the Heartbeat of God

My Prayer from the Heart

Heavenly Father,

Forgive me for those times when I haven't encouraged and taught new believers. Forgive me, also, for times when I've allowed legalistic and judgmental attitudes to keep me from trusting that You are their God, not me. Teach me the fine balance of discipling and encouraging, while still pointing new Christians to You, the faithful Shepherd. Help me to encourage new believers to be connected to the Body of Christ, while firmly abiding in the Vine, developing a strong relationship with You. Give me faith that as I teach and encourage believers to abide in You, there shall be much fruit—both in their lives and in the Kingdom of God.

In Jesus' name,

The Lord's Answer/s to Me

_____

_____

_____

_____

EPILOGUE

THE HEARTBEAT CONTINUES

As you now complete this series of devotions, I pray that it has forever changed your life. Close your eyes for a moment and listen. Have you learned to hear the heartbeat of your heavenly Father? Do you see His outstretched arms reaching out for souls? Can you see that our Father really does hold the whole world in His hands and in His heart?

Now, think of your daily walk with Jesus. His heartbeat reflects the Father's heart. As you abide in Christ and allow Him to be your Savior and Lord, you will discover that your heart will also reflect the Father's. To gauge your progress to that end, ask yourself these questions :

- Have I become more aware of the harvest fields my heavenly Father has placed me in?
- Have I learned to ask Jesus to help me to reach out to people, trusting in the Holy Spirit to guide my prayers, my words and my actions?
- Do I rely on the power and fullness of the Holy Spirit to help me faithfully and boldly witness to people about Jesus?
- Do I willingly give my time to respond to the Holy Spirit's prompting to seek out and minister to the lost?

Awakening to the Heartbeat of God

- Do I pray and declare God's Word regarding the harvest fields in my life?
- With faith, have I learned to recognize the harvest?
- Have I become familiar with scripture keys for sharing the Gospel, which brings the power of God unto salvation?
- Who has been drawn closer to the Lord as a result of my witnessing and obedience? (List them)
- How do I now help new believers grow in their relationship with Christ?

I trust that your heart is now beating stronger for souls. Even more, I trust that you realize that our heavenly Father's heart is beating for *you*. His love, compassion and tender mercies are new for *you* every morning. Know that you are accepted in the beloved, a child of the King, and that He invites you to be an ambassador for His Kingdom, ready and willing to introduce many to our Lord and Savior, Jesus Christ. If you accept that call, take His hand and begin reflecting His love to the world around you, for surely His heartbeat continues.

Ministry Page

I pray that this book has inspired and equipped you to respond to God's heartbeat for souls. As you reach out to the people in your harvest fields, trust that the Lord of the Harvest is already there, compelling you to witness for our Savior. And may God bless you with the joy of seeing many experience the miracle of His salvation!

For more information about obtaining this book, in single or bulk quantities, as well as obtaining other inspirational material by the author, contact:

**Susan Skelley at
heartbeatofgod@clearwire.net**

or

**Glory Bookstore
Daytona City Church
211 Bay Street
Daytona Beach, FL 32114-3235
info@daytonacitychurch.com**